WORLD WAR ME

Volume II:

I DESIRE

Presented To:

_____

From:

_____

Date:

_____

WORLD WAR ME

Volume II:

I DESIRE

DR. JAMAL HARRISON BRYANT

DESTINY IMAGE® PUBLISHERS, INC.

P.O. Box 310, Shippensburg, PA 17257-0310

"Promoting Inspired Lives"

This book and all other Destiny Image, Revival Press, MercyPlace, Fresh Bread, Destiny Image Fiction, and Treasure House books are available at Christian bookstores and distributors worldwide.

For a U.S. bookstore nearest you, call 1-800-722-6774.

For more information on foreign distributors, call 717-532-3040.

Reach us on the Internet: www.destinyimage.com.

ISBN 13 TP: 978-0-7684-3912-0

ISBN 13 Ebook: 978-0-7684-8953-8

For Worldwide Distribution, Printed in the U.S.A.

1 2 3 4 5 6 7 8 9 10 11 / 13 12 11

DEDICATION

I dedicate this book to my daughters: Topaz, Naomi, Grace, Angel, and Adore. My desire for you is God-prepared men who are better than your dad.

Endorsements

Dr. Bryant gives the readers permission to have desires, yet gives them the key to not allowing their desires to have them by offering solutions which empower the reader to focus their inner promptings toward permanent victory and blessing. This is a must read for those who want to transform their longings into all that God wants them to be.

Michelle McKinney Hammond
Author, *Why Do I Say Yes When I Need To Say No?*

This book, *World War Me* takes responsibility for its author's weakness while reminding us that satan seeks each of our demise. It gives distinction between weakness and wickedness which is often sutured together as one reality in the minds of people.

BISHOP T.D. JAKES SR.
Potter's House of Dallas

Dr. Bryant's book helped me realize that life is not a game, it's a battle zone! Every man who is serious about living will come to the conclusion that you can still make the touchdown after you've been tackled by life. This is a must have playbook for making better decisions

DEION SANDERS
Retired NFL Player/
NFL Network Sports Analyst

CONTENTS

FOREWORD

The issue of desire is something seldom explored in church, yet it remains the elephant in the room for most believers. The struggle between the flesh and the spirit, the war between the pull of the world and the still, small voice of God, tears at the heart and mind of most who are striving to be all that God created them to be. Desire is good, but it can also be bad! For many, knowing how to lift and separate personal longing from divine inspiration can be a daunting task. We vacillate between pondering what Jesus would do while still making impulsive, bad choices with far-reaching consequences, and simply doing nothing, becoming so spiritual that we are of no earthly good. Should we follow our hearts or use our heads?

The answers can be elusive when the seductions of our own desires overwhelm us.

I can think of no one more able to tackle this issue than Dr. Jamal Bryant. Not only is he a skilled orator, but his ability to separate fact from fiction and make the spiritual practical is a gift which promises to transform all who are privy to his teaching and wisdom.

Not only is this a guide that readers can comprehend and apply to their lives, but it is literally a roadmap to help the readers navigate through the challenges of desire to a place of mastering them and gaining the victory which they so deeply desire to experience in their lives. Dr. Bryant gives the readers permission to *have* desires, yet gives them the key to not allowing their desires to *have* them by offering solutions which empower the reader to focus their inner promptings toward permanent victory and blessing. This is a must read for those who want to transform their longings into all that God wants them to be.

MICHELLE MCKINNEY HAMMOND
Author, *Why Do I Say Yes When I Need To Say No?*

PREFACE

King David declared forthrightly, *"One thing have I desired of the LORD, that will I seek after..."* (Ps. 27:4 KJV). I so marvel at David because he is the only person I know to have made such a bold claim and accomplished it. There are so many natural human needs—the need for affection, the need to be affirmed, the need to be empowered, and the need to be embraced. In other words, David meant that he didn't have any of those needs or desires.

Most of us have desires, whether legal or illegal, godly or ungodly, secular or sacred, we all have many desires. How then do we channel our energy from destructive desires to empowering desires? The aim and scope of this book is to help us redirect our desire. Not long ago, I had a problem with my car and the battery went dead because I left the lights on. I asked a passerby, "Can you give me a jump?" Something strange happened. He pulled out cables from his trunk, connected them to his car, and then connected them to mine. There was transfer of energy. His car needed energy to move, my car needed his energy to be turned on. The desire was the same, but the place was different.

Most of the things we do in sin are natural desires that have been corrupted through carnal consciousness. It is my hope that our mind frame will line up with the will of God so that our desires will be godly desires and not demonic desires.

INTRODUCTION

No matter what age you are, you have desires. If you desire the same thing at 40 that you did when you were 10, then your desire is dysfunctional. Likewise, if you still want the same things now as you did before you were saved, then your desires are misappropriated. There is a tension of desire called conflict and crisis of desire. For example, a drug addict may hit rock bottom and want to get away from the substance and lifestyle that has stripped him of his family, finances, job, and self-esteem. While going through the healing process, his desire may tempt him to use drugs again, so internal conflict ensues because his consciousness has shifted.

The same thing happens when you grow up in the *Kingdom*. Just because you are saved doesn't mean you will not desire things that are unethical.

In Romans 7:18-19, 24, Paul said,

> *I know that nothing good lives in me, that is, in my sinful nature. For I have the desire to do what is good, but I cannot carry it out. For what I do is not the good I want to do; no, the evil I do not want to do—this I keep on doing... What a wretched man I am! Who will rescue me from this body of death?*

Do you desire something that will satisfy your flesh or something that will satisfy your faith? When David was on the balcony, he saw Bathsheba bathing across the street and fell into temptation to fulfill the desire of his flesh. Nathan, the prophet, showed up and asked him why he had risked his title and relationship with God in trying to feed the appetite of his flesh. David then understood that he could no longer make the flesh his first priority:

One thing have I desired of the LORD, that will I seek after; that I may dwell in the house of the LORD all the days of my life, to behold the beauty of the LORD, and to enquire in His temple (KJV).

Chapter 1

PRINCIPLES OF DESIRE

One thing I have desired of the LORD, that will I seek: That I may dwell in the house of the LORD all the days of my life, to behold the beauty of the LORD, and to inquire in His temple (Psalm 27:4 NKJV).

A *desire* is a hunger, a craving, a preoccupation, or an internal aim for an external conquest. In one word, a *desire* is a *wish*. For example, as you read this book, you are experiencing the fulfillment of a desire. Even if you are reading at the behest of someone else, you are fulfilling the desire to please that person.

It is strange that people are *not* taught how to desire. Desire can be fulfilled without practice. Sickness and old age do not diminish desire; they just change the objects of your desire.

You have to be in a vegetative or a complete meditative state to stop desiring, and even then, you have to set the intention not to desire.

> *"Falling in love is the paradigmatic example of desire"*
> **—William Irvine**[1]

In the different stages of growth, a human being has different desires. A baby girl's desire may be milk, a dry diaper, and warmth. As she grows into a little girl, she may desire attention and acceptance. When she becomes a woman, she desires affection, and as she matures into an elder, she desires assistance. In the male world, things are a little different. A boy's desire may be centered around things, like toys, building blocks to construct a castle, and later a gun to shoot the castle down. As a young man, he may desire power, money, friends, and great success in his career or business. As he approaches his prime and matures, he desires a mate and wants to leave an unforgettable legacy to his children. As you see, neither age nor gender matter. Desire plays a key role in all of our lives at every stage. If at 40 your desire is still the same as it was when you were 10, your growth in consciousness must have become stunted.

In life, we decide for ourselves what to desire. When we become born again, our desires ought to be different from what we desired before we were saved. If our Christmas lists as saved people mirror the same lists that we had when we were not saved, that means our desires may not have changed or matured.

Society, today, teaches that to achieve happiness and fulfillment, we have to change our job, hairstyle, wardrobe, spouse, income, and other external factors. But God urges us to change internally in order to be happy and fulfilled. We do not think up desires; they are formed in us.

The greatest example for understanding desire is falling in love. Two people go on a date for the first time. Their intentions may be to just get to know each other and have a wonderful evening. However, if one of them wakes up the following morning in a bed that is not their own, that person may be humiliated, embarrassed, and even shocked. In the initial plan to go out on a date, he or she probably had not planned on having sex.

According to William Irvine, falling in love is, in fact, an act of going against our will.[2] Lust is different in terms of desire, because it can be fulfilled with any willing participant. But when you fall in love, there is an object of your affection that no other person can replace.

God urges us not to put people on pedestals and give them high expectations as if they were gods. God says, *"If you love Me, why don't you stay up at night trying to figure out where I am?"* God does not want us to have an extreme desire and love for other people, a love that may look like it is beyond our love for Him. It is unfortunate that we claim to love God, but live our lives with divided attention.

God is interested in our total love. He wonders why we say we love Him, yet live very distracted lives. Our attention is divided and our love capricious. The lack of love is almost as fleeting as its existence. Sometimes it is like the wind: You don't know where it is coming from, and you don't know where it is going.

Let us look at the concept of desire in another way. Sometimes people go broke due to uncontrollable desires manifested through negative spending habits. Are you broke? Examine the spending habits in your life and calculate how you got that way. Did you end up broke over the things you desired?

Why do we desire to own a car that may not be utilitarian to our needs? It is amazing that some people do not buy clothes simply because they like the color or style. Some have been influenced by magazines such as *Cosmopolitan, Vogue, XXL,* and *Essence.* Others may be influenced by America's Next Top Model. Many of them have been co-opted into believing, "I have to dress like somebody else." Why would we desire and buy clothes that do not even fit us right or express who we really are?

We build for ourselves our own branding and advertising mechanism that sounds like, "I have to dress a certain way, drive a certain car, or live in a certain kind of house, not because I want these things, but because it is a status symbol in America."

But what happens after your desire to get the SUV is fulfilled, but you can't afford to buy gas? Or your desire for a house is fulfilled, but can't afford the heating bill. You might get the clothes you so badly desired, yet can't pay off the credit card bill. These are examples of extreme desire. Extreme desire makes us throw away resources that God has given to us.

You will notice that when desire is over-stretched, it leads to bankruptcy. As a consequence, the average American in an average month doesn't save anything, but borrows on credit to support a lifestyle that is commensurate to his or her desire.

Where do our desires come from? Our desires come from an evolving experience in our lives. Many of us do what psychologists call *overcompensating.* When we were growing up, our parents may not have been able to buy us a certain label or brand of shoes we wanted. Now that we are grown up and make our own money, we remember that when we were 11 years old, we dreamt we would buy whatever shoes we wanted. We end up with closets that we can't even get into because we have more shoes and clothes than we need. All this has come about because we are trying to fulfill an unfulfilled desire that was birthed in us when we were 11 years old.

CRISIS VS. CONFLICT OF DESIRE

There is a difference between the crisis of desire and conflict of desire. The crisis of desire can be likened to the ways of a drug addict. Addicts enjoy getting high until they hit rock bottom. Something inside their nature prompts them to give drugs up, and they say, "These are killing me. I have lost my family, job, friends, and resources. I don't want to do this anymore, but something in me still yearns for the drug."

Paul the apostle said that sometimes when we should be doing good, evil steps in our way. Being born again does not make us immune to sinful desires. In fact, when one gets saved, it can be very difficult to keep away from sin. In some instances, it seems that the urge to practice the bad habits increases the more one tries to stay away from them. It is absurd that some folks claim they never have a desire to do anything that is unholy. As human beings, we may time and again need God to get ahold of us. We love God, but there are other things that we like, too. If God doesn't keep us, the desires of our flesh will become greater than the desires of our spirits.

Nicholas James Vujicic is an extraordinary motivational speaker who was born without arms or legs, but with two small feet, one of which has two toes. He overcame his disability to live not just independently, but a rich, fulfilling life, becoming a model for anyone seeking true happiness. Nick tells the story of his physical disabilities and the emotional battle he endured trying to deal with them as a child, a teen, and a young adult. "For the longest, loneliest time, I wondered if there was anyone on earth like me, and whether there was any purpose to my life other than pain and humiliation."[3]

Being one of the first disabled students to be integrated into a mainstream school in Victoria, Australia, he learned to write using the two toes on his left foot, learned to use a computer, throw tennis balls, play drum pedals, comb his hair, brush his teeth, and answer the phone. In his recent book, *Life Without Limbs*, he writes:

I'm officially disabled, but I'm truly enabled because of my lack of limbs. My unique challenges have opened up unique opportunities to reach so many in need. Just imagine what is possible for you![4]

During The 700 Club interview, Nick narrated,

My dad was saying that his head was next to my mom's head as I was being born. He saw my shoulder. He just went pale. He was hoping my mom didn't see me, because he saw that I had no right arm. My dad had to leave the room, and he couldn't believe what he saw. The doctor came in, and my dad said, "My son has no right arm." [The doctor] said, "No, your son has no arms or legs." And he said he nearly fell on the floor. He couldn't believe it.[5]

Later, Nick narrates:

The whole church was mourning, like, "Why would God let the pastor's son be born that way?" My mom, at first, didn't want to hold me. She didn't want to breastfeed me. She just felt very uncomfortable for the first four months. It took them quite a while before they could trust in God that He didn't make a mistake—that He didn't forget them or me.

I wanted to end it. If God wasn't going to end my pain, I was going to end it myself. So at age eight, I tried to drown myself in a bathtub with four inches of water. I told my mom and dad, "I'm just going to relax in the bathtub. Can you put me in the bathtub?" I turned over a couple of times to see if I could do it. I couldn't.

The thought that stopped me from going through with it was the love for my parents. I loved them so much, and all they did was love me. I pictured my funeral. I pictured my parents, and all I saw was guilt on their shoulders that they couldn't have done more. I thank God that He didn't answer my prayer when I was begging him for arms and legs at age eight. Because guess what? I have no arms and no legs, and He's using me all around the world.[6]

We all have different desires. For instance, I don't want to die before my purpose is fulfilled. I don't want to die crazy, broke, stressed-out, or run amock. My desire is to please God. My plea to God is, *Don't take me until I have done everything that You want me to do in life.*

There were some things that I used to like to do when I was 20 years old that are different from what I liked to do when I turned 30. Along the way, I have been through some experiences that have changed me. They have made a man of me. Like iron sharpens iron, they have sharpened my intellect and attitude. I am no longer impressed by petty, shallow, insignificant happenings. My desire is to live a life of substance and value. That being said, I am not easily impressed. My desire is to say, *God, not my will, but Your will be done.*

When we go through the crisis of desire, there are various things we encounter. There is the loss of the ability to desire. This comes from being very terrified by the negative consequences of some of the desires in one's life.

Usually, one's desire doesn't really change until it has turned its head. One may desire a person very much. He or she may even go ahead and get acquainted with that person. However, after knowing this person, he or she may regret having ever desired this person. People end up praying, *God, please take that desire away from me, because I know that loving this person is going to kill me.*

Most people, if they are honest, will testify that this has happened to them. However, we have to grow to a point where, if we acknowledge that someone is not good for us, we will let them go. We will ask God to help us love them without desiring them in a way that is not healthy for us.

The second principle is the conflict of desire, in which you may become disgusted by the very thing you desire. The same intensity with which you desire may be the same intensity by which you feel disgust. One of the many ways people can measure maturity in faith is to realize that there were things they used to like which were a liability to their lives and by which they now are repelled. They may simply have been living a life without any restraint or discretion, doing anything at anytime, anywhere, and with whomever they pleased. Yet looking back now, the very sight of some of those people and things disgusts them.

Some people look back over the stuff they used to like and say, "What was I thinking? What was on my mind?" Have you ever been sick of your own mess? Have you ever not been able to look at yourself in the mirror? But now you are able to say, "Since God has changed my desire, look at me—I am a testimony. I didn't make it on my own, but somebody prayed for me."

Then there is a "change of life" desire. As we go along, our lives and desires change. Many singles are carefree and footloose. At this stage in life, they could desire some things that would otherwise be unheard of in a parent. However, if people want the same things as parents that they did when they were only responsible for themselves, there is a possibility that their desire is dysfunctional, and something ought to be done about it.

Similarly, if people are married, but still desire some things or activities that they wanted while single, their desires here could be seen as dysfunctional. The same goes with salvation. If, in fact, you are saved, but still desire the same things as when you were running in the streets, it means you have not grown up yet. That is why somebody sang, "The things I used to do, I don't do no more; places I used to go, I can't go anymore." Let me take it a step further: I have two hands. They are the same hands. However, I am using them to do different things than I used to. I used to touch and take stuff with them, but now when I look at my hands, I say, *"Father, I stretch my hands to worship You."*

Siddhartha Gautama, the founder of Buddhism, was a part of the elite class in India. His father, who was one of the richest men at that time, wanted him to have such a sheltered life that he kept his son in the palace until he was 27 years old. He didn't want him to see sickness, disease, or poverty. At 27 he got permission from his father to venture out on his own.

He was excited, "Let me see the world, because I don't want to be in this isolated vacuum," he said. When he walked out of the palace, he saw all of the poverty and disease that was among the people. He was so horrified that he took a vow of poverty. According to him, all the riches he'd had just insulated him from seeing the doldrums of despair. He renounced his wealth because of its contrast to the abject poverty in which most people lived.

Sometimes God has to take you outside of your comfort zone to give you another perspective. Many times, after close scrutiny, you will find that you didn't really need the things you thought you needed. He may also want to show you that the grass which seemed to be greener is not really as green as it appeared. God may want you to stop and say, "I wanted all of this, but now that I have it, it is not doing me any good."

If you have not done so already, you will soon discover that the Christian faith is a journey. Wherever we are, we can often stop to say, "I have come this far. Desire didn't change until I got what I wanted. And when I finally got what I wanted, I realized that there was still a void and emptiness in my life. I realized that I don't need all that stuff to make me happy."

King David was one man who had his share of ups and downs. Psalm 27:4, like many others, was written by him.

> *One thing have I desired of the LORD, that will I seek after; that I may dwell in the house of the LORD all the days of my life, to behold the beauty of the LORD, and to enquire in His temple* (KJV).

A few days prior to writing Psalm 27, David was walking around out on his balcony. He looked across the street and saw a fine woman named Bathsheba whom he had never seen before. His heart was wide awake. He said, "You know what? I desire that. I want her." So he sent his henchmen. "Go bring her to me, because I desire her." He slept with her and got her pregnant. She was married, so he orchestrated a plan to have her husband killed (see 2 Sam. 11:5-27).

Nathan, God's prophet, went to David and confronted him. Nathan was trying to figure out David's choices. Was David sane? With all the anointing and the favor that was upon his life, how could he throw everything away because of the desires of his flesh? He told David that God could take away his kingship, his title, and his position because he had allowed the desires of his flesh to overrule his desire to know God.

Maybe you have made poor choices as a result of wanting to fulfill the desires of your flesh. In Psalm 27:1, David says, *"The Lord is my light and my salvation—whom shall I fear? The Lord is the strength of my life—of whom shall I be afraid?"* David's longings changed from flesh to favor because he realized what God meant to him. It is not until you have a divine and close encounter with Him that you understand who God is.

My one desire is to see the beauty of God's Holiness. I pray that your desires will start to change. God says that you can live without the things you thought you could never live without.

ENDNOTES

1. William Braxton Irvine, *On Desire* (New York, NY: Oxford University Press, 1952).

2. *Ibid.*

3. Nicholas James Vujicic, *Life Without Limbs* (New York, NY: Double Day, 2010).

4. *Ibid.*

5. Nicholas James Vujicic, interview, *700 Club* (June 29, 2009).

6. *Ibid.*

Chapter 2

THE PEOPLE WE DESIRE

WHY DO WE DESIRE
CERTAIN PEOPLE?

Everyone wants to be loved, admired, and respected. However, after being hit with some of the harsh and painful experiences of life, a lot of people have given up on having these desires ever fulfilled. Some people have relinquished the yearning to be admired, and they believe that it is futile to think they will be respected. But at the end of the day, if they haven't received the love, respect, and admiration they need, at their core is still the desire to be acknowledged. *The Invisible Man*[1] is a book that changed African-American literature. It explored the idea that people can walk through life while their very existence is ignored by others. Innately, God created us with a need for other people.

This need surpasses basic needs—water, food, and oxygen. Some people would rather go without food than go without people. Prolonged isolation breeds a level of insanity. William James, a philosopher from Great Britain, said, "To be alone is one of the greatest evils that you can inflict on another human being." Consequently, about 100 years ago, the penal system instituted the understanding that if you place a man in solitary confinement, he will be left to his own wits and find himself coming to the brink of insanity. We *need* people to affirm our very existence. They help us know whether we have put on weight or lost weight, whether our hair is a mess, if our outfit matches, or whether we are losing our grip on life. Others help us to affirm who we are.

> *"To be alone is one of the greatest evils that you can inflict on another human being."*
> **—William James**

We need people for interaction, conversation, satisfaction, and self-actualization. We really don't know who we are until somebody else has, in fact, sealed our own identity for us. Recently I was invited to lecture at Kentucky State University in Frankfurt, Kentucky, at a time when something strange was happening there. One hundred miles outside of Louisville, Kentucky, people were in a state of emergency, because they were operating out of a practice called "gift sharing." I was shocked to discover that out of this trend, people who live in poverty were trying to contract HIV/AIDS on purpose because they wanted to get attention and benefits that they may not get through welfare. Something happens when people need people. In Baltimore City, 13-year-olds try to get pregnant just to birth somebody who will depend on them and love them.

Three thousand years ago, Marcus Tullius Cicero, the great Greek philosopher, wrote that even the philosophers who argued and wrote against fame and popularity still signed their names in doing so.[2] Even the philosophers who said they were against popularity wanted to be recognized. It was, in fact, Tacitus, another Grecian philosopher, who wrote, *"The lust of fame is the last thing that a wise man shakes off,"*[3] because at our core we all sing the melody of the theme song to the popular '80s sitcom, Cheers: *"You want to go where everybody knows your name."* I want to go where I can be recognized and validated, where I can be sealed into my identity.

Some Jews who went around driving out evil spirits tried to invoke the name of the Lord Jesus over those who were demon possessed. One day an evil spirit challenged the seven sons of Sceva, saying, *"Jesus I know, and I know about Paul, but who are you?"* (Acts 19:15). God's anointing on our lives is so intense that even demons recognize who we are.

For thousands of years, little girls in Israel stood on tiptoe in anticipation that they would be selected to carry the seed of Abraham. This seed would be the manifestation of the prophetic proclamation of Isaiah, that there would be somebody born who would be wounded for our transgressions, bruised for our iniquities, and by whose stripes we would be healed (see Isa. 53:5). Young girls growing up in Israel, beginning at 12 years of age, probably looked each other in the eye and said, "I wonder if you are the one who has been selected to bear The Lord." You will know that you have been selected when God keeps opening doors you didn't ask for or delivers you from things which held you captive.

You may have registered success in your life, even through very strange circumstances. You could have run wild in the streets and smoked weed, but you still have brain cells. You could have slept with little Dottie and everybody else available, but you are still HIV negative. This can help awaken you to the fact that you have been chosen for such a time as this.

God is determined to make your name great. He didn't say He was going to make your face great. In other words, folks may not recognize you, but they will know you. When God changes who you are, people no longer recognize you. If you were broke and messed-up and God changes your status, it would take people awhile to recognize you, because they would be in shock. God will make your name great so that folks will recognize the God who is in you.

Whenever you hear somebody you don't even know talking about you, don't check them; instead, tell them, "Thank you for putting my name out there, because the next time you hear about my name, I will be great." God is doing something for your name. Never shun that which used to be attached to your name. God had to get your name out there for free publicity, so that when people hear that you have been blessed and you have walked into your wealthy place, they will scratch their heads in disbelief and ask, "Is this the person who used to sell drugs?" or "Is that Susie, who was always in the club?"

You have to be delivered from the opinions and approval of other people. If you live for other people to validate you, the same people who inflate you will have the power to deflate you. You have to know that you are great and that you look good, even if no one tells you. If you haven't been on a date in seven months, you can take yourself out.

It was John Paul Sartre who said, "Hell is other people."[4] Hell is living for other people, because I have found out that the more you try to make other people happy, the more you will make yourself miserable. No matter what you do, they will find something else to be dissatisfied about. If you learn to love yourself, you will not care about the people who leave your life.

Living for other people has the capacity to consume you. High school students wear jackets to let other people know that they "lettered" in track. After graduation, they get a tattoo to let somebody know a characteristic about them that is not seemingly obvious. When they get their first car, they want personalized tags so that someone following behind them, whom they don't even know, will know who they are. Throughout life, people fight for recognition, but not for Christ who lives in them. Make up in your mind not to dress or live for other people. If there is one person whom you ought to turn on or impress, it should be the Lord through your praise.

Here is a test as to whether or not you are living for other people. What would your desire be if you were left in the world all by yourself without the existence of any other person? How would you dress? What kind of house would you want to occupy? What kind of car would you aspire to drive? What kind of worship would you desire to give to God? Whenever we come to worship, God expects us to ignore the crowds and to act as if it is just us and Him.

When the LORD saw that Leah was not loved, He opened her womb, but Rachel was barren. Leah became pregnant and gave birth to a son. She named him Reuben, for she said, "It is because the LORD has seen my misery. Surely my husband will love me now." She conceived again, and when she gave birth to a son she said, "Because the LORD heard that I am not loved, He gave me this one too." So she named him Simeon. Again she conceived, and when she gave birth to a son she said, "Now at last my husband will become attached to me, because I have

*borne him three sons." So he was named
Levi. She conceived again, and when she
gave birth to a son she said, "This time I
will praise the LORD." So she named him
Judah. Then she stopped having children*
(Genesis 29:31-35).

In Genesis 29, we are introduced to a young
lady by the name of Leah. Although she was,
in all accounts, always loyal to Jacob, the sen-
timent was not returned to the same degree.
Jacob actually loved Rachel, Leah's younger
sister, and they were intended to be married,
but because of the custom that the older sister
must be married first, Laban, Leah's father,
resorted to a wedding night switch in the dark-
ness. In the morning, Jacob discovered that
Leah had become his wife. Laban then permit-
ted Jacob to marry Rachel, as well, a week later.

Leah had a son named Reuben and knew
that her husband was going to love her again;
he loved her for a moment and went back to
Rachel. She conceived a second time and had
a son named Simeon. She knew, this time, that
there was no way her husband was going to
ignore her the second time. She had a third son

by the name of Levi and believed that, since she'd had three sons, naturally, her husband would love her. But the husband had other plans. After the third son was born, her desire shifted. She was reluctant to spend emotional and physical energy on a man who obviously was not interested in her. She decided to have a fourth son whose name was Judah. This is what was on her mind, "The first three I did for a man, but this one I am doing for God."

Living for other people has the capacity to consume you.

Judah means "praise." God doesn't want us to praise Him just because we need something from Him. He would like that we praise Him just to let Him know we can't live without Him. When I go to church, I have one thing on my mind: I will enter into His gates with thanksgiving in my heart and into His courts with praise (see Ps. 100:4). We all need to praise God, especially if we have something on the inside of us that says, *God, I owe You praise. I owe You praise because of something You did in July; You made a way in August; You paid a bill in October, and I have come to give You glory. I just can't stop praising Your name, because if I don't praise You, then the rocks will cry out. I don't want any rocks crying out for me.*

Let everything that has breath praise the Lord (see. Psalm 150:6). We shouldn't be inactive when we ought to praise God. How can we be silent when God has paid our bills, has awakened us this morning, has given us a right mind? We have every reason to praise the Lord! In Psalm 27:4, David says

> *One thing I have desired of the LORD, that will I seek: that I may dwell in the house of the LORD all the days of my life, to behold the beauty of the LORD, and to inquire in His temple* (NKJV).

When you woke up this morning, there should have been only one thing on your mind—how you were going to act in His presence, not questions concerning what you were going to wear or who you were going to sit next to throughout the day. You should have asked yourself, *How am I going to respond when*

I know that, if it had not been for the Lord on my side, I would be nowhere?

When you do an etymological exploration of the word *Christian,* you will find it means "Christ-like"—so those who are saved have Christ in them. That is why you can't write off people based on what they look like. The Word of God says you shouldn't get weary of welcoming strangers, because some did this and welcomed angels without knowing it (see Heb. 13:1-2).

The way you treat the least of these is the way God will treat you. God is not going to bless you until you mature to the place where you can bless someone else. You need to bless those who do not have what you have and especially those who believe in the God whom you believe in.

When you have a desire, you don't need a manual. Nobody tells you how to get your fix. If you know what you need and how you like it, then you know how to get it. Praise God without anyone telling you how to do it. You don't need to have a guitar, a keyboard, or a microphone. Praise God just because of who He is to you. My desire is to enter into God's gates with thanksgiving and His courts with praise. I beseech you to praise God as if you are desperate for Him and as if you can't live without Him.

ENDNOTES

1. Ralph Ellison, *The Invisible Man* (New York, NY: Random House, 1995).

2. Reid, James S: *M. Tulli Ciceronis pro A. Licinio Archia poeta ad iudices: edited for schools and colleges* (Cambridge University Press, 1897)

3. *Ecclesiastical History* iv., 6.

4. Wallace Fowlie, *Dionysus in Paris* (New York: Meridian Books, 1960) 173.

Chapter 3

PERSISTENCE OF DESIRE

Do you desire to be better? Then something has to change in your vocabulary. Your psychological disposition has to change, too. You need to shift away from wishing. Some of our thoughts may sound like these: *I wish I was a millionaire; I wish I owned my own business; I wish I lived in a different kind of house; I wish I could shift my life from depression; I wish I had more friends; I wish I could shout and be exuberant like other people.*

※ A wish is the longing to have something you would like happen to you when you least expect it to. Have you ever considered a wish as your vision and your vision as a launching pad for desire? Whenever you stay with a wish list, you stay out of the faith realm. When your faith becomes connected to a wish, it becomes a desire. And your desire is manifest through a prayer and an action. Do you still wish for a better life without praying for it to happen or sacrificing for it to manifest?

As a Christian, I don't wish that something would happen by accident. I desire God to do something inside of me so that I can be part of His work. God expects to hear a positive language from us. You shouldn't just want something to happen to you, but you should expect the best for your life. When I wish for something, I refer to myself, but when I desire alongside the will of God, I address Heaven to reorder and redesign my life.

When your faith becomes connected to a wish, it becomes a desire.

You move from wishes to the realm of desire when you often think about your desires. God does not want you to merely wish. If something only crosses your mind occasionally, you don't really want to have it. But if you eat, sleep, and drink thinking about something that you want, then it becomes urgent. Every day seems like a longer day because you will not be satisfied until you get what you want. When you are determined to get something, you will spend a lot of time calculating and trying to figure out how you can achieve your desire. While other people settle for the average, people with desire will dream of how to shift their finances.

God is interested in seeing how defiant you can get, to the extent that you will not be detoured when somebody else doesn't believe in the manifestation of your desires. There are people who know that, naturally, certain things are not theirs. However, they have so much faith that they will not rest until they have obtained what they want. Their faith will not let them rest. They don't know how it is going to happen, but God promises to grant the desires of their hearts.

Matthew 9:27 says, *"As Jesus went on from there, two blind men followed Him, calling out, 'Have mercy on us, Son of David!'"* Though the blind men couldn't see, they heard Jesus was passing. They started screaming, because they knew that when He showed up, they would get what they desired most—sight. This they knew Jesus could give.

When you see somebody emphatically praising God, it is not necessarily because their desires have been met, but because they are anticipating that their need is about to be met, or they are very sure that the One whom they have trusted will not let them down. I am not sure of the kind of sound blind people make when their blessing is coming.

Let me paint the picture: The blind men are sitting by the roadside, and they hear Jesus coming. When His footsteps are heard on the dusty road, their desire to see becomes even stronger, because they won't be able to see until they get to Him. The lesson we can learn from this is that if you can get to Jesus, whatever you desire will happen.

Matthew 6:33 says, *"But seek first His Kingdom and His righteousness, and all these things will be given to you as well."* When you desire the things of God first, God will let you see the things you couldn't see. God tests you, to see whether you want Him more than the things you desire. When God tests you, the purpose is to prove that your faith is real. It's not that

God needs to prove it to Himself, since He knows all things; rather, He is proving to you that your faith is real, that you are truly His child, and that no trial or test will overcome that faith.

The blind men detect that Jesus is coming. When He gets close, they start screaming; *"Have mercy on us, Son of David"* (Matthew 9:27). Some of the onlookers who do not share the blind men's desire to see, try telling them to be quiet. The irony is, all those who are telling the poor, blind folk to be quiet can already see! They can't understand why these blind fellows are screaming that loud. These people, unlike the blind men, have everything.

You have to understand that the people who are irritated by the sound of your worship are not in need of what you need. If you want your need to be fulfilled, you will not care about other people's opinions. You will have one thing on your mind, *I have to get my desires met!* You have to have so strong a desire that no matter what anyone says, no matter how they try to talk you out of it, you will still make your stand, and, like the apostle Paul, you will be able to say, *"I know whom I have believed"* (2 Timothy 1:12).

You have to have a desire because the adversary has desires as well. In Luke 22:31-32, Jesus told Peter,

> *Simon, Simon, Satan has asked to sift you as wheat. But I have prayed for you, Simon, that your faith may not fail. And when you have turned back, strengthen your brothers.*

Like Peter, we are constantly on the devil's mind. His desire is to cut us in half so that when we feel like we are falling apart, he will have conquered. I can't give the enemy that victory, because he wants me to break down, be depressed, and feel like I am at the end of my rope. God, in His Word, exhorts us to remain strong. When we feel like we are falling apart, we need to get it together.

We must desire to live and not die. We have come too far to let the enemy destroy our families, minds, or spirits. The devil desires to make us feel like we are falling apart, but God loves us so much that He prays for us not to fail. Hebrews 7:24-25 says,

Jesus lives forever, He has a permanent priesthood. Therefore He is able to save completely those who come to God through Him, because He always lives to intercede for them.

Jesus lives to intercede for us, so we will not get depressed, feel inadequate, or lose our minds, because the devil's assignment is to sift us like wheat.

Job 1:8-12 says,

Then the LORD said to Satan, "Have you considered My servant Job? There is no one on earth like him; he is blameless and upright, a man who fears God and shuns evil."

"Does Job fear God for nothing?" Satan replied. "Have You not put a hedge around him and his household and everything he has? You have blessed the work of his hands, so that his flocks and herds are spread throughout the land. But stretch out Your hand and strike everything he has, and he will surely curse You to your face."

The LORD said to Satan, "Very well, then, everything he has is in your hands, but on the man himself do not lay a finger." Then Satan went out from the presence of the LORD.

The devil does not want to mess with *you*, because God has done a wonderful job in protecting you. He has built a hedge of protection around you. Like He did with Job, the Lord decided to lower the hedge around you so the enemy can try messing with you a little. However, the Lord knew the devil would not be able to break you.

The principle is this: Anyone who asks for permission to do something does not really have the authority to do the same. Therefore, the enemy does not have any authority, because he has to miserably beg for permission to mess with you a little. I thank God that the devil's season is over. Maybe he tried to kill you, but you are still standing, because the Lord could not let the enemy touch you.

Some time later, Jesus went up to Jerusalem for a feast of the Jews. Now, there is in Jerusalem near the Sheep Gate a pool, which in Aramaic is called Bethesda, and which is surrounded by five covered colonnades. Here, a great number of disabled people used to lie— the blind, the lame, the paralyzed. One who was there had been an invalid for thirty-eight years.

When Jesus saw him lying there and learned that he had been in this condition for a long time, He asked him, "Do you want to get well?" "Sir," the invalid replied, "I have no one to help me into the pool when the water is stirred. While I am trying to get in, someone else goes down ahead of me."

Then Jesus said to him, "Get up! Pick up your mat and walk." At once the man was cured; he picked up his mat and walked... (John 5:1-9).

This portion of Scripture in the book of John gives us a wonderful picture of desire. According to this chapter, there was someone with desire at the pool called Bethesda. According to ancient biblical tradition, the troubling of the water at the pool of Bethesda only happened once a year, and whoever was the first one in the water would be the very first one to get healed. The disabled people sat by the pool, waiting for the water to stir. The water at the pool can be used as a metaphor for the Holy Spirit. So they had to wait for the moving of the Holy Spirit, and whoever jumped in first, no matter what the affliction was, they got healed.

Whatever your desire is, God will meet your need only if you learn how to worship Him wherever you are. You can tell how desperate people are from the way they are quick to praise God.

The pool can be compared to a church with several people getting healed, getting new jobs or new cars, getting married, operating in their gifts, and flowing in the Spirit. However, some people remain seated by the pool with unanswered prayers. Those with unanswered prayers made the right choice when they decided not to quit.

The question that God poses for you is whether or not you desire a better life. "Do you desire to just sit by the pool for the rest of your life, or do you desire to walk again?

Do you desire to be strengthened, to walk in your purpose, to know your gifts, or to know the better plans for your life?" He asks.

When Jesus saw this man lying there and learned that he had been in this condition for a long time, He asked him, *"Do you want to get well?"* *"Sir,"* the invalid replied, *"I have no one to help me into the pool when the water is stirred. While I am trying to get in, someone else goes down ahead of me."* Christ did not ask him what kind of background he came from or whether he was a Christian. All Christ wanted to know was if the man wanted to get well.

I ask you, "Do you desire to be a better believer? Do you want God to speak directly to you? Do you desire to be able to open up the Scriptures and have them come alive right in your home?"

The man at the pool had been sick for 38 years. The Bible does not say why this was so. The text says that Jesus knew about it. This was Jesus' first visit to Bethesda. Theologians suggest that Jesus only lived for 33 years. By the time Jesus visited the pool, he was probably 30 or 31 years old. This could mean that seven years before Jesus was born, he looked down from Heaven and saw the man at the pool who had a desire. When Christ showed up at the pool, it was a sign that all the time the man had spent praying for healing had not been in vain.

God knew what you were dealing with before you were saved. He knew what your struggles would be long before you were born. God had to wait for you to get in the right environment, where miracles manifest. He has what you need, and He wants to know if after all these years you still trust Him to deliver you.

Then Jesus said to him, *"Get up! Pick up your mat and walk,"* and at once the man was cured; he picked up his mat and walked. You may say, "I can't walk," but God's view is, "Yes, you can! Get up and start walking, but don't walk by yourself." When you walk, carry what you used to depend on, so that the world will know that you have achieved victory over the things which had bound you. You will not be ashamed of codependency, because God will have picked you up.

You need to be independent, inspired, and involved in order to get your desires met. Jesus didn't pick the lame man up. He wanted him to get up on his own and to believe that when he arose, no weapon could bring him down.

For desire to be met, you must have initiative to do something which no one else has ever told you to do. Maybe part of your frustration is that you don't have any role models to show you how to do the things that God put in your heart. God supports this state of affairs in your life because He doesn't want you to look to people. He wants you to look to *Him*. God desires to give you insight into parenting your children. He would like to show you which way to go and how you should run your business. However, you have to show initiative and have the ability to take a step.

The pool of Bethesda was surrounded by sick people. Everyone there had a different issue. They were at the place of miracles and healing, and they all had a desire.

Before Jesus got to the pool, there was a great deal of tension, because only one person would get healed in a year. Each time the pool water stirred, there was a scramble to get into the water first and to receive healing. After Jesus left the earth, there was no need for the pool. No longer do we have to wait for even a single moment each year to get into a pool or be jealous of somebody else getting there before us, because Jesus is not working it out for just one person. He is doing it for whoever is at the "pool" and still believes. It may be getting cold outside, but the "pool" is open, and those who are trusting God will have their desires come to pass. God can fulfill the desire of every person at the same time. Just jump into the "pool" and say, "God, I trust You."

At our "pool" today, many people need jobs or solutions for their children in crisis. God is no respecter of persons. All you need to do is trust and believe Him; He can meet your desire. Your desire might not be the same as your neighbor's, but you both need God.

Chapter 4

PSYCHOLOGY OF DESIRE

Oh LORD, You deceived me, and I was deceived; You over powered me and prevailed. I am ridiculed all day long; everyone mocks me. Whenever I speak, I cry out proclaiming violence and destruction. So the word of the LORD has brought me insult and reproach all day long. But if I say, "I will not mention Him or speak any more in His name," His word is in my heart like a fire, a fire shut up in my bones. I am weary of holding it in; indeed, I cannot (Jeremiah 20:7-9).

According to John Eldredge, desire is the source of our most noble aspirations. It is also the source of our deepest sorrows.[1] Pleasure and pain come from the same region—the heart. Simone Weil, a noted philosopher, said that there are only two things which pierce the heart: Beauty and Afflictions.[2] There are moments that we wish would last longer, and there are moments that we wish had never even started. The choices we make are a reflection of what it is we desire in pleasure. We choose or select based on the desire of our hearts. The desires in our hearts (spirits) stem from our minds.

There are two different approaches to life. The first approach is the need to do things out of duty. The second is the longing to do things out of desire. The former can cripple the soul. If you do everything out of duty, you may never understand your desire. There was a man who came to church and lost his sense of purpose. He was faithful to the church, active in the ministry, and a participant in every program. When asked why he was so active in the church, he said, "It is what I am supposed to do." When you do anything out of duty, you lose your sense of desire.

> *"There are only two things that pierce the human heart: Beauty and Affliction."*
> **—Simone Weil**

Do not follow God because you think it is what you are supposed to do. You have to follow God out of passion and a desire to do it. As long as you are doing something to please someone else, you will never be fulfilled. When you get to a place where you are doing everything out of desire, you find fulfillment. The psychologist, Daniel Gilbert, says that we have a tendency to badly want things, and then get them and realize that we don't need them. He calls this "miss want."[3] What I want for my life ought to be driven by my desire. It would not be enough for me to merely want something, but never go after it. That would not make it a desire, because it has no drive.

Desire, in itself, is like momentum or a motor. What is it that is driving you? Do you have a desire for a better life? Do you desire to be a better person, parent, husband, or wife, or is your heart only after material things? If you just want material things, then you don't have a desire to do better. A person who always wants something, but has no desire to make it happen, will not encourage you to have a drive toward your own destiny. At some point, as adults, we have to outgrow the "Peter Pan Syndrome" of dreaming that things will work out without us having to put forth any effort to make sure that they actually do happen.

You could have been praying and seeking God. However, after you got off your knees, there was nothing that showed you were serious about what you desired. Something is wrong with immature believers who, in fact, believe that they can shout and become debt free without making some sacrifice. God says, "If you want something to happen, you can't expect Me to give you breakfast in bed and do the dishes." There has to be a work component connected to desire.

Something has happened to our generation, today. We have raised a generation of children who are wishers and not dreamers. When we deal with children, we have to show them that, depending on the situation as it arises, there really is cause and effect. Children must know that in life, we do not always get what we want just because we ask for it. Sometimes, as a parent, you have to say, *No!* and say it forthrightly.

As parents, it does not hurt to face a child who is asking for something and say, "I am not giving it to you, because I can't afford it, and you don't need it." There ought to be some knowledge in us that tells us that giving children anything they want and whenever they want is destructive, as it does not at all prepare them to know that, in the real world, they will find that some doors are closed.

What, then, do people do, after doing everything that it took to acquire what they thought they needed so badly, and upon getting it, they realize that it was not what they needed after all? There are people who have desired something, and when they finally fulfilled that desire, they felt let down because they thought that the fulfillment of it would be the final need. They said things like, "If I can get this, I will be happy."

In life, desire should be backed up by trying. Trying out something helps us get what we want, and once we get it, we can then develop a liking for it. However, the question is, what happens when we get something we really desired, but after we get it, we are still unhappy?

Attitudes must change in the Body of Christ. We have to change the way we think and how we do things. We need to realize that material possessions do not satisfy us.

No matter what kind of car I have, if I don't have anywhere to go, it is useless to me. It doesn't matter what kind of house I am living in or how much money I am making; if I don't have peace of mind, sanity, and joy in my heart, everything is a waste. Most times, people who make less money and have never been to college are the very epitome of happiness. The reason such people are happy is because they've found out that they don't need things to validate who they are. They've learned that all they need is to have a relationship with God. This gives them ultimate fulfillment.

In effect, when we lose things, we will not lose our minds, because *we* have found out that we can be happy without all the material possessions. Therefore, we know that we can make it with or without all the things we crave. We can get everything and still be miserable.

People who have been through difficult situations cease to be impressed with material and tangible things.

Sometimes this can cause mixed reactions toward you. Real, mature believers are not those who can praise God when they have it all. They are people who can shout when they don't have all they may want, but they know that the Lord is still making a way for them.

When your desires and wishes change, your maturity level changes, too. Your maturity level changes because your mind changes. God is not only interested in your heart, but in your mind as well—the ability to reason.

Maybe there were moments when you have thought about suicide or "jumping over the edge," but God tapped you on the shoulder and said, "Don't you dare think about it. Do you think I took you through all of that just so you can go crazy now?" God preserves you just to instill perfect peace in your mind.

Even if we desired the things we wanted, we would not be sure of total happiness. We can make a security deposit in the things that we so desire, thinking that if we got them we would be totally happy, but the truth is that we would still be insatiable. This is because of a psychological phenomenon called *adaptation*. It is the belief that what we get ceases to satisfy us after we have become used to it. When we first get something, we are excited, but after it has been around us for too long, familiarity creeps in and brings forth contempt.

The possible reason as to why God could meet a portion of our needs and leave out others is that He does not want us to take His grace for granted. Seasons of spiritual drought are to create a spiritual hunger in us, so that when God finally shows up, we are grateful.

There are many people who feel permanently unfulfilled, in that, no matter what they get, they are still unhappy. We often meet people like that. They seem to have it all together, but they still complain. They are mad about everything; they are always in a bad mood, and they have a nasty attitude. It is deplorable and despicable that we walk away from them drained, trying to figure out what they want. Such people are evil, nasty, and cantankerous. They are an enigma. The harder we try to figure them out, the madder they seem to appear.

I have heard women say, "I don't have any girlfriends. I can't deal with other women because they are petty, jealous, and messy." That is a wrong statement to make as a woman. Isn't it absurd for one to say that she does not trust women, and yet she is one? Part of the problem is the tendency to generalize issues. Clearly, not all women are petty, for instance. One may have been unfortunate to meet someone who was, who had no positive desires, and so couldn't find fulfillment in herself.

Computers run programs with excellence, precision, and accuracy. However, a computer can't work in a vacuum. Ultimately, the only way a computer can run a program is through a hard disk. You have to understand that God-given desire works like an engine in your system. Your mind reasons, and your intellect formulates ideas. You were created to dream and to live to see those dreams come true. You are not inert. There is something that naturally pushes you to excel.

Some of our "desire systems" have been attacked by a virus. This renders us dull and lifeless. People with infected "desire systems" are hopeless and pessimistic. Unhappy with themselves, they get sick of seeing someone else run, and they get tired of seeing busy people, so they urge them to slow down, advising, "You are doing too much." Most times, the people saying these words are those who do nothing. We must get up and refocus. We have to get connected with people who can motivate us to be the best that we can be.

There was a man who had been a member of our church family for a couple of years. He was very intuitive, highly intelligent, a successful business leader, a wonderful husband, and a great father. A few years ago, he ended up at Johns Hopkins to undergo brain surgery for a tumor that was growing on his brain. When he went in for surgery the third time, the surgeon removed a piece of his frontal lobe, which is connected to the neuron system of emotions in the human body. That changed his life forever. This gentleman retained the ability to think, but lost his sense of feeling.

Soon after this incident, the man lost his job because he couldn't follow through on an assignment. He would start an assignment, but halfway through, his mind would meander to something else. His emotions were not connected to the urgent situation that affected his life. Due to the fact that an important part of his system was affected, he could not use his intellect and will to complete the assignment.

It is the same with us. When we lose focus on our purpose, even when we have not undergone surgery, it is as if we have lost a piece of our mind. People lose their minds when they can think but not feel, because the two go hand in hand. There are so many people who are too analytical, trying to figure out why they are doing what they are doing. Such people don't release their hearts to not just think through the situation, but also to feel through it. It pays to use our emotions to get some assignments in our lives accomplished.

God has put you in a circumstance where your E.Q.—Emotional Quotient overrides your I.Q.—Intelligence Quotient. There are some people who, when they go to church, expect to receive only a sermon and then return home. They reason that they don't need to express themselves by shouting and screaming. They frown at those screaming, and they wonder,

"Why are they carrying on and screaming like that?"

The reason could be simply that people who praise God by expressing themselves loudly have to go beyond a place where they can think to a place where they can feel. If you were to ask such people why they are shouting, they probably couldn't really give you a logical answer. Depending on what issues they are dealing with, it could well be a natural emotional reaction. The prophet Jeremiah said that when he tried to sit still it felt like fire shut up in his bones.

> *Oh LORD, You deceived me, and I was deceived; You overpowered me and prevailed. I am ridiculed all day long; everyone mocks me. Whenever I speak, I cry out proclaiming violence and destruction. So the word of the LORD has brought me insult and reproach all day long. But if I say, "I will not mention Him or speak any more in His name," His word is in my heart like a fire, a fire shut up in my bones. I am weary of holding it in; indeed, I cannot* (Jeremiah 20:7-9).

There are things that will break you more than they make you. Sometimes it is quite ironic. You may ask God for something, and He answers your request. You may be shocked, however, to discover that after getting what you yearned for, thinking that it would give you fulfillment, it almost drives you out of your mind. Jeremiah knew he had the gift of prophecy, but he couldn't sleep at night. People talked about him all the time. They scorned him because of what he was prophesying. Every time he spoke, he felt like he was getting ready to die. Being tired of it all, Jeremiah finally halts and says, "I will not speak or make mention in His name."

Like Jeremiah, we sometimes halt. We tell ourselves, *The next time I go to church, I am going in there with my arms folded and my lips zipped up, and I am not going to cause a scene.* When we get to church, however, something else happens. By the time we go through the service, something has changed. We may find ourselves in another mode. We get excited and a little stirred up for action. It may seem like something is tugging at our toes. The tingle may slowly make its way up to our knees. Before we know it, it is in our stomachs, and before we come to ourselves, we have opened up our mouths and given God His Glory. Like Jeremiah said, "His word is in my heart like a fire, a fire shut up in my bones. I am weary of holding it in; indeed, I can not."

ENDNOTES

1. John Eldridge, *Desire* (Nashville, TN, Thomas Nelson Inc., 2007) 11.

2. Simone Weil, *Gravity and Grace* (New York, NY, Putnam, 1952) 206.

3. Daniel Gilbert, *Stumbling On Happiness* (New York, NY, Knopf, 2006) 129.

Chapter 5

PARTS OF DESIRE

There is reason to believe that we have multiple sources of desire within us. The 18th century philosopher, David Hume, said that our desires are an ongoing wrestling match between "ought" and "is."[1] Our desires cause internal friction or tension between the way things are and the way we would like them to be.

- People who are complacent, or satisfied with life, have temporarily lost the ability to desire. However, when you are caught in a predicament, there is something which pushes you from the way things are toward the way things ought to be. When your desire is less for the way things ought to be, you have resigned yourself to an attitude which says, "I am satisfied with the way things are."

The two sources of desire, argues David Hume, are "Emotion" and "Passion"—which is the ability to feel bad or good mentally or physically, and the intellect—the source of thought.[2] Some of our desires have nothing to do with feeling, but are based on our thoughts.

The Ancient Greeks adopted the Ancient Kemetic (Egyptian) proverb, "I think, therefore I am."[3] What you think about ought to give you a strong desire. People who never think about another way of life have no desire, because their thoughts are not in a greater place. Sometimes desire is born out of determined thought about having something greater in life. The last thing the enemy can steal from you is your desire to think about a better life. If you didn't think about how things could be better, then the enemy would have, in fact, taken the victory.

"I think, therefore I am."
—Ancient Egyptian Proverb

This is what God says concerning desires that are trapped in our thought system. *"My thoughts are not your thoughts, neither are your ways My ways..."* (Isa. 55:8). This means that, contrary to your beliefs, your thinking may be keeping you from happiness. But, if you think the way Christ thinks, you will learn how to be content at all times. Philippians 2:5 reads: *"Let this mind be in you which was also in Christ Jesus"* (NKJV). When you are saved, there should not only be a change of heart, but also a change of mind.

Desires are formed out of emotions—the motor that drives us. Our emotions are our motivation. Emotions and motive come from the same Latin word, *movere*, which means "to move." We can, therefore, deduce accurately that any person who does not have a desire is not motivated. There are people in our society who can't do anything because they are not motivated. It could be a child, spouse, friend, or neighbor. The only way that we can want more for our lives is to desire it.

People who bask in what they have now, living with the impression that what they own now and where they are is the plateau, usually end up losing the much-needed desire for even greater things, which is the power behind success. The enemy will hoodwink you into believing that you have reached the lofty heights of success just because you have a certain kind of car and are living in a particular neighborhood. You may even have approval or validation from certain people.

Stop a moment and reflect. That is the enemy trying to draw you into satanic success. That may not be God's idea of success. According to God's Word, success is the understanding that when you get to level one, you will inquire of the Lord, "God, is this all that you have for me?"

If we don't fulfill desire, which is emotionally oriented, we feel bad because we have missed the opportunity to feel good. Our desire is driven by the prospect or the possibility of two different operations. My desire is to bring myself pleasure, but when my desire matures, the things that used to bring me pleasure cease to be that significant, because the things that I used to like no longer motivate me. The other reason could be that I have a deeper desire that goes beyond something that is tangible and superficial. When I move to the place of maturity, I tell God, "You don't have to bless me with just some material possessions, even though they are good, because I desire something spiritual."

I don't need intellectual stimuli to obtain an emotionally invoked desire. When you experience hunger or pain, you don't need your intellect to figure out what is happening. Emotions make you aware that you are hungry. As soon as you take food, even without thinking much about it, the hunger will stop. Understand that emotions have an unfair advantage over your intellect. If somebody walks up to you and says something cynical, sarcastic, or crazy, your emotions don't know what has just been said.

It takes your intellect to process the fact that they just tried to offend you; then your emotions take the signal from your intellect. You then judge the situation, and a thought process may emerge that sounds like, *What am I going to do about this? Am I going to give them a piece of my mind, or am I going to remain quiet and not go down to their level?* If the perpetrator says something that your intellect doesn't comprehend, you can't be offended, because you don't even know what they were really saying and what their intent was. So your intellect has to be in a place like, *I'm not sure what you said, but I can tell that you are trying to get over on me.*

> **"Let this mind be in you which was also in Christ Jesus."**
> **—Philippians 2:5 NKJV**

Maybe you are attending a meeting where people are talking over your head. Then, quietly, something in your spirit whispers to you that it is time for you to put up your prayer radar. You may begin to sense something is not right and the thought comes to you, *There are things in this legal document I can't process, but I know that someone is trying to get the best of me.*

This is called discernment. Through discernment, people can understand that there are some things in their emotions that their intellect doesn't understand and, hence, avoids. Maybe that is too philosophical. Let me break it down. At one time or another, there was probably a person in your life who tried to get close to you. You didn't know what was wrong with the person, but there was something in your spirit that said, *Stay away from this person, because what this person has is not healthy for your spirit.*

INTELLECT VERSUS EMOTIONS

There is a tension between our intellect and our emotions. Let us say, for example, that I am going to California over the holidays to visit my parents. The fastest way for me to get there is by plane. I can get on a plane and be in Los Angeles five hours from this very moment. My intellect knows that it is the most expeditious and convenient way. But with my emotions, things may be a little different. If I am afraid of flying, I may fail to get on the plane.

Now here is where we have a problem, because the enemy tries to mess with our emotions even when he is aware that God has given us the information. There are things that God has birthed in us that He wants us to desire, but our hearts are afraid to get on the "plane."

When you deal with the tension between intellect and emotion in the realm of your desire, you will find an easy test to see where emotions take over and where your intellect stops. In a private moment, let your mind tell your body to hold its breath for one minute. For 15 seconds it will not be a problem, for 30 seconds, not an issue, but after 40 seconds, your emotions will start to throw a tantrum. Your emotions will appear to say, *We can't do this; let it go.* Your body is not really in danger, but your emotions will send you into panic or survival mode. Since you are bound to listen to your emotions over your intellect, you will let your breath go.

Emotions have the capacity to fight unfairly because they are like a spoiled 5-year-old child. If they don't get their way, they start kicking and screaming and rolling around on the floor. In order to get their children to sit down and not embarrass them in public, some parents give children what they want so that they will stop acting like *clowns*. Emotions act the same way. When you don't give the flesh what it desires, it will start rolling around acting like a *fool* until it can get what it wants. God doesn't care how much you kick and scream. He will not give you what your flesh is screaming for, because He knows that it is not good for you.

You have to understand now how to deal with *your* emotions when they act like a spoiled 5-year-old. When you have such children, you can put them in their bedrooms, punish them, or spank them. But when your emotions act up, there is nothing that you can do to them but pray that God will change you.

The prophet Jeremiah got a twisted desire. His intellect and his emotions were in two different places. He wondered why God called him to preach. All hell had broken loose in his life since he started preaching. He remembered that God had promised to protect him if he submitted himself (see Jer. 20:7-9).

Just like Jeremiah, we may feel shocked that we still experience situations that can make us emotionally charged. We think, *I thought that after I got saved I would not have to go through the attack I am going through right now! God, You played me. I thought that after I diligently gave my tithe, I would not have to deal with all the people who hate me. God, I am not going to say anything else for You. I am not going to shout anymore.* Listen to Jeremiah's experience:

But if I say, "I will not mention Him or speak any more in His name," His word is in my heart like a fire, a fire shut up in my bones. I am weary of holding it in; indeed, I cannot (Jeremiah 20:9).

In verse 9, Jeremiah's emotions became greater than his intellect. He realized that when he wants to shut up, there is something inside of him that feels like fire! In other words, Jeremiah had an acute case of "I can't help it."

Your intellect may begin to say, I am too gentle and sophisticated to be screaming while praising God. I come from too good a background to be lifting up my hands in worship. However, every time I try to sit down and act sophisticated, something that is in me begins to rise up.

There was some stuff that God put me through this year that didn't make sense. Have you ever been at a place where you were mad at God and you were vehemently saying, "I can't believe that God allowed me go through some of the mess I have been going through? Why did He have to let me be this broke?" And God said, *"What are you thinking about; you think that you are calling the shots? You don't even understand that I had to take some stuff from you in order to get some stuff to you."*

Jeremiah's emotions were so intense that they could only be likened to fire. Fire consumes and it burns. When you catch the fire, God will start to burn your previous desires so that what you previously desired you don't like anymore. I no longer go to places I used to, because wherever there is a fire, anything that is flammable, anything that gets close to it, will burn.

ENDNOTES

1. *Hume, David. A Treatise of Human Nature: A Critical Edition, David Fate Norton and Mary J. Norton (eds.),Oxford University Press, 2007. Book 3, Part 1. 294.*

2. *Ibid.*

3. Descartes, René. From Discourse on Method, July 1, 2008 [EBook #59], http://www.gutenberg.org/files/59/59-h/59-h.htm#part4

Chapter 6

PROBLEM OF DESIRE

I do not understand what I do. For what I want to do I do not do, but what I hate I do....For what I do is not the good I want to do; no, the evil I do not want to do— this I keep on doing....What a wretched man I am! Who will rescue me from this body of death? Thanks be to God— through Jesus Christ our Lord! So then, I myself in my mind am a slave to God's law, but in the sinful nature a slave to the law of sin (Romans 7:15,19;24-25).

I want to argue forthrightly that I am rather upset with the apostle Paul. Don't get me wrong; I think that he wrote some things of great value. It was Paul who eloquently wrote, *"I press on toward the goal to win the prize for which God has called me heavenward in Christ Jesus"* (Phil. 3:14)

It was Paul who wrote profound truths such as, *"The One who is in you is greater than the one [satan] who is in the world"* (1 John 4:4). Paul is a wonderful writer when dealing with salvation. In his letter to the Romans, Paul wrote, *"If you confess with your mouth, 'Jesus is Lord,' and believe in your heart that God raised Him from the dead, you will be saved"* (Rom. 10:9). He even gave fashion tips:

> *Therefore put on the full armor of God....Stand firm then, with the belt of truth buckled around your waist, with the breastplate of righteousness in place, and with your feet fitted with the readiness that comes from the gospel of peace...take up the shield of faith...take the helmet of salvation and the sword of the Spirit, which is the word of God* (Ephesians 6:13-17).

He was an excellent writer who wrote clearly so that everyone would understand the theology of God and not just the life of God.

Paul, the ex-gang-banger-turned-Gospel-globetrotter, wrote more works than any other apostle or disciple. But in Romans 7, neither Paul nor I benefit, because he gives us an appraisal without an antidote. Paul shows us a problem, but he doesn't give us the prescription. I am somewhat dismayed with Paul, because he does what so many preachers do. Paul tells me what's wrong with me, but then doesn't teach how to get it right. When I attend church, I don't want preachers to tell me what's wrong with me without telling me how I can change. In church, we encounter a sword through the Word, but it all depends on who is holding the sword. It's either a butcher or a surgeon. A butcher will chop you into pieces, while a surgeon will slice you, but sew you back up.

A butcher will slice you into pieces, while a surgeon will slice you, but sew you back up.

As human beings, we have come to a place where we no longer want to just look at what's wrong, but we also want to find out how to make it right. As we read through Romans 7, we hear a litany of Paul's complaints and gripes, not about the church at Ephesus, Corinth, or Galatia, but surprisingly about himself. It sounds almost dismal and seems impossible when we consider the personhood of Paul—who had been saved by God, was very intelligent with many degrees, but took up a whole Bible chapter to tell us what was wrong with himself without telling us how we could correct those things in ourselves. In Romans 7:15-18, Paul doesn't understand himself because he repeatedly does what he never intends to do.

In the same Scripture, Paul shares that it doesn't matter how saved you are, because there's something you're always going to wrestle with on the inside of you. You are never going to get to the place of healing and recovery until you stop looking at what's wrong with other people and admit that there is some stuff broken in you that needs to be fixed. Even Narcotics Anonymous believes that the first step to recovery is admitting that you have a problem.

When you get to church, don't act as if there is nothing wrong with you, because church is like a hospital, not a museum. Your issue might be low self-esteem, and another person's issue might be pride. Or your issue might be greed and another's, drugs, but all attend church because they believe Jesus can fix all issues at the same time.

Every religion in the world addresses the issue of desire—some as a heavenly ambition, and others for earthly tranquility. For example, we could analyze Buddhism, a religion founded by a young man named Siddhartha Gautama, who was a son of an Indian warrior king and lived from 566 to 480 B.C. Gautama led an extravagant life through early adulthood, reveling in the privileges of his social caste. But when he got bored of the indulgences of royal life, Gautama wandered into the world in search of understanding. After encountering an old man, an ill man, a corpse, and an ascetic, Gautama was convinced that suffering lay at the end of all existence. He renounced his princely title and became a monk, depriving himself of worldly possessions in the hope of comprehending the truth of the world around him.

There is no crown without the cross, no blessings without sacrifice.

The basic document of Buddhism deals with absolving oneself of pleasure; it is called *The Four Noble Truths*. They are the Truth of Suffering, the Truth of the Cause of suffering, the Truth of the End of suffering, and the Truth of the Path that leads to the end of suffering. More simply put, suffering exists, it has a cause, it has an end, and it has a cause to bring about its end. The concept of pleasure is acknowledged as fleeting. Pursuit of pleasure attempts to satisfy what is ultimately an unquenchable thirst. The same logic belies an understanding of happiness. In the end, only aging, sickness, and death are certain and unavoidable.[1]

God desires us to have pleasure; however, suffering is a part of life. We could not celebrate Easter had there not been a crucifixion. The problem with many of us is we don't understand that God is not going to give us the

Crown without giving us the cross. We keep hungering after blessings when we don't want sacrifice. When we are living through sacrifice, know that there is a blessing attached. If God were to just give us blessings, we would be spoiled.

The Buddhist religion is built and based around suffering, and it argues that by overcoming desire you have overcome suffering. In a nutshell, Buddhists believe that everything is subject to change and that suffering and discontentment are the result of attachment to circumstances and things that, by their nature, are impermanent. In Buddhism, by ridding oneself of these attachments, including attachment to the false notion of self or "I", one can be free of suffering.

My argument with this thought is that there are many people who don't want anything for themselves, yet they still struggle. The devil wants you to be satisfied with where you are, because for you to be content means that you are no longer expectant.

According to Buddhist theology, they ascribe an eightfold plan as a pathway to handle desire. *The Noble Eightfold Path* describes the way to the end of suffering, as it was laid out by Siddhartha Gautama. Together with *The Four Noble Truths,* it constitutes the central meaning of Buddhism. Great emphasis is put on the practical aspect, because it is only through practice that one can attain a higher level of existence and finally reach *Nirvana.* The eight aspects of the path are not to be understood as a sequence of single steps; instead, they are highly interdependent principles that have to be seen in relationship with each other.

They believe that one has to have the right view, the right intention, the right speech, the right action, the right livelihood, the right efforts, the right mindfulness, and the right concentration. My observation is that many people *say* the right thing, *have* the right intention, *do* the right thing, *live* the right lifestyle, *make* the right efforts, but they still haven't made progress. What happens when you keep doing the right thing, but you see people who are still doing the wrong thing and going past you?

Another sect of Buddhism is Zen Buddhism. The teachings of the Buddha have, to this day, been passed down from teacher to student.

Around A.D. 475, one of these teachers, Bodhidharma, traveled from India to China and introduced the teachings of the Buddha there. In China, Buddhism mingled with Taoism. The result of this mingling was the Ch'an School of Buddhism. Around A.D. 1200, Ch'an Buddhism spread from China to Japan, where it is called (at least in translation) Zen Buddhism.

Out of Taoism, there are no prescriptions to deal with desire because the basic philosophy of Zen Buddhism is, "The more you know, the less you speak, and the less you speak is a sign of the more you know." The problem with so many of us is that we talk too much when we don't know anything. The elders are believed to say, "If you are ignorant, nobody knows until you open your mouth." Stop giving people advice when you don't even know how to handle your own marriage or raise your own children.

When you deal with the template of Zen Buddhism, they do not have what Islam calls the Koran, but they have the Koan, which deals with the realm of the astrological or the illogical. Koans often appear as paradoxical or linguistically meaningless dialogs or questions.

It is within the religion of Zen Buddhism that people will spend years studying the principle; for example, what is the sound of one hand clapping? It is within the monastery of Zen Buddhism that they will spend years in contemplative meditation: Who will hear the sound of one tree falling in the forest, if no one is there to listen to it?

God doesn't want you to deal with the illogical, the stuff that will blow your mind and not make any sense. God will not put you into a monastery for you to spend countless hours trying to figure out the sound of one hand clapping. Instead, God is interested in knowing the sound of someone who is blessed with two hands clapping and praising Him.

Christianity is not about being or having, but about desire. There ought to be a desire in every Christian that doesn't reflect what the world desires. There ought to be something in you that says, "I want more than fame, wealth, and popularity." Solomon, the wisest man who ever lived, was given an option to declare whatever he wanted, and God would grant it to him:

At Gibeon the LORD appeared to Solomon during the night in a dream, and God said, "Ask for whatever you want Me to give you."...[Solomon answered,] *So give Your servant a discerning heart to govern Your people and to distinguish between right and wrong. For who is able to govern this great people of Yours?* (1 Kings 3:5,9)

Solomon did not desire wealth, notoriety, or military strength, but instead asked for wisdom. He knew that if he got wisdom, he could control the entire world. Wisdom is better than education, because there are a lot of people who are intellectual graduates who lack common sense.

In Romans 7, Paul declares that the thing he struggles with is sin. It's sin because sin made him desire things that are holy in an unholy way. Sin makes us desire things that are legally ours before our ordained time. For example, sex is not a sin, because God wants us to have good pleasure. God designed us to desire sex, but He expects us to wait until we get the right person because His Word is clear on this issue—sex is intended for marriage, not before, but after (see Eph. 5:3-5; 1 Cor. 6:9-11, 18-20; Rom. 6:11-13; Heb. 13:4). Money is not a sin; it is the love of money that will corrupt the purest of hearts (see 1 Tim. 6:10). If our whole lives revolve around how much money we need to make and how we will get paid, it's then that we have put our priorities in the wrong place.

Paul says of his own admonition, "When I would do good, evil steps in my way" (see Rom. 7). In other words, the thing he liked was the thing killing him. You don't have to be delivered from something you don't want or something you've never experienced. Anybody who says that being holy is not a struggle is a liar. Salvation is *work*. It's easier being a sinner than walking away from some evil things that you enjoy. All you can say is, "God, the only way that I can walk away from it is if You do it for me."

In Second Corinthians 12:7-9, Paul gave an addendum to Romans 7:

> To keep me from becoming conceited because of these surpassingly great

> *revelations, there was given me a thorn in my flesh, a messenger of Satan, to torment me. Three times I pleaded with the LORD to take it away from me. But He said to me, "My grace is sufficient for you, for My power is made perfect in weakness...."*

The issues that Paul was wrestling with were in his flesh. Our greatest fight is over the things we can feel.

For example, you've never had to wrestle with God to get a car off your mind. The 16th century theologian, John Calvin, admonished that in order to deal with and live through something that's killing you, you have to learn how to pray.[2] If you pray while you're in pain, your pain becomes pleasure. While Paul struggled with the thorn in his flesh, three times he prayed to God to remove it. God didn't, probably to see if Paul would mature with the pain. Maybe you've asked God to remove some people from your life, but they are still there giving you trouble. God may not take them away, so that every time you feel the pain, you know that it's for His glory.

> *It's in moments of trial that*
> *God demands worship more*
> *than in moments of triumph.*

Every time you feel tempted, weak, and vulnerable, the sure way to get the devil out of your space is to begin to worship. *It's in moments of trial that God demands worship more than in moments of triumph.* When you are triumphant, God demands praise, but when you are in trial, He needs worship!

Paul kept trying to do good, but ended up doing bad. The only thing that could get him to his desire was if he gave his mind to God. Your body is a slave to desire, but if you give your mind to God, you'll have a perfect balance. You can only deal with the desires that conflict with your integrity if you surrender your mind to God, and not to the Buddhists' *Four Noble Truths*, which absolve people of pleasure.

ENDNOTES

1. *Basics of Buddhism, Thailand, Jewel of the Orient, the living Eden,* video (PBS Home Video, 2000).

2. John Calvin, *Calvin: Institutes of Christian Religion 2*, (Philadelphia, PA, Westminster Press. 1960) 855.

Chapter 7

PURSUIT OF DESIRE

After Jesus was born in Bethlehem in Judea, during the time of King Herod, Magi from the east came to Jerusalem and asked, "Where is the one who has been born king of the Jews? We saw his star in the east and have come to worship Him" (Matthew 2:1-2).

In my studies of world religions, I discovered that the oldest Hindu scripture, the Veda chant known as *Rig Veda*, written in 1500 B.C., ascribes that before God made light, the very first thing He created was desire.[1] This is contrary to what the sacred Bible states. According to Genesis, the book of creation, desire was the very last thing God created.

There are three pivotal and fundamental miracles in the creation story:

- God's creation of something out of nothing

- The creation of matter

- The ability to seek

In matter, flowers had the ability to open and to close, single-celled animals were able to replicate themselves, an atom was able to spin, and light was able to beam. Out of all the things created in matter, their activity was not predicated on desire, but instead activated out of duty. None of the single cells or atoms did anything as a result of desire.

Many people go through life operating in jobs, relationships, and environments simply driven by an overwhelming sense of duty or responsibility. God created us to fulfill our desires, not to live under the yoke of obligation. Whenever you are on a job because the job pays rent, it is not the maximum desire God has for your life. God wants you to be in a place where you are being fulfilled.

Probably you are connected to somebody whose relevance in your life has expired. Milk is healthy until the expiration date. After the expiration date, it begins to stink and will contaminate everything it touches. Any relationship to which you feel you are obligated is not healthy. God loves for people to be connected to Him, not out of duty, but out of desire. I encourage people not to attend church merely to appease the person who dragged them there. Rather, people should have the desire just to be in the presence of God.

The third miracle in Genesis was the ability to seek. It is therefore a miracle that people are able to desire something when there are millions of people who are just happy with mere existence. They are not looking for anything in life, but are content with the way things are in the present. Everyone should know that there is more to life than what they have, and God has impregnated them with a desire.

You know you are selected for desire when God impregnated you with a desire you did not desire for yourself. The sign that it is a desire from God is when it neither lines up with the things in your background nor matches what you wanted for yourself. It becomes hard to explain to other people why you want what you want when you only know that there is something in you that you can't resist.

There is little wonder the devil will try to corrupt your desire by assigning demoniacs and friends to try to talk you out of your vision, which the Lord placed in you. When God puts something in you, you don't need people to validate or support you; you only need to have the assurance that it will never die. A true God-given desire, dream, or vision takes God to bring it to manifestation. Maybe there is something that you want from God, and you know that in the natural it won't come to pass, but if you believe in the supernatural, there is no way it will fail.

When God was about to send Jesus to save humanity, the archangel Gabriel appeared to Mary and told her she was highly favored of God to give birth to the Son of the Most High. Mary's response was, *"May it be to me as you have said"* (Luke 1:38). In other words, she knew that whatever God had in store for her was destined to come to pass. Immediately after her remarks, her womb opened and the seed was deposited.

When you open yourself to the will of God, every God-given desire will unfold in your sight. The impetus of desire is so acute and paranormal that when God puts a desire in you, it will drive you to formulate plans to achieve or obtain it. When you have a desire or craving for someone, you can get up at 3 A.M. and drive nine miles. Desire will cause you to achieve whatever it is you want.

Marvin Gaye's lyrics were so poignant that Kelly Clarkson had to sing them again:

> *"Ain't no mountain high enough,*
> *Ain't no valley low enough,*
> *Ain't no river wide enough,*
> *To keep me from getting to you..."*[2]

Look over your life and think of the crazy stuff you used to do just to get fulfillment from people. God demands the same attention. Get up extra early and seek His face. In the middle of the night, just call out His name because you have a desire to seek Him.

> **When you have a desire or craving for somebody, you can get up at 3 A.M. and drive nine miles.**

Your environment dictates what you desire. Sunflowers are heliotropic plants whose heads turn all day long in the direction of the sun because they have to face it in order to survive. Pine trees excrete a sap when animals and insects try to eat off their bark so that the creatures will become entrapped and entangled, and their bark will not be eaten. When a paramecium runs into an obstacle, it will turn around and go in the opposite direction rather than be stopped. The sunflower, the pine tree, and the paramecium do these things for survival, not out of desire.

Some of the things you did were not because you wanted to do them, but because you needed to do them in order to survive. Your environment dictates your desires. If you are living in a mansion sitting on 13 acres of land, your desire is not for God to give you space, but if you are in a cramped two-bedroom apartment with 13 kids, you need a "Jabez anointing" to enlarge your territory (see 1 Chron. 4:10). Don't let people assess your desires based on theirs, because needs differ. As a result, when I shout to God and you get irritated, it is proof that you are not as desperate as I am. So I won't require your approval to determine my level of praise or the intensity of my desire.

Your environment speaks to your desire. It is hard, then, to get excited for overflow when you need cash flow. Some people can afford to be caught up in the trappings of church because they are looking for extra. However, when you desperately desire basic necessities like help with rent, car, phone bills, or getting your hair done, you won't let people determine your praise and worship.

There is but one bridge between my current state and my changed state, one path connecting where I am to where I want to go, one thing to get me from my current profits to my antici-pated income desire. Desire is the determina-tion not to settle or be content with what you have. Be grateful for your blessings, but make up your mind to continually seek God's hand for even greater goodness to flow.

To have this desire, physiologists and neurologists concur that there is something built into every person called "reflexology." A reflex is an action or decision that cannot be controlled. This, therefore, means that desire may cause you to do things beyond your control, simply as a response to its force.

When you have a complete physical, the doctor will have you sit on the table and tap your knee. Instinctively, or out of reflex, your foot moves out. You do not consciously instruct your foot to do this, nor does your heart "feel" like doing it, but as soon as the knee is tapped, there is a reflexive response.

That is what God builds in every believer. God will tap you the right way until He gets the right praise out of you so that you don't have to think about it before doing it. If you have been through multiple hurts and pains, you will not wait for an organ; you will simply praise God as a reflex. Probably, you are in pain right now, but you still have praise; you are frustrated, but you still have praise. Reflexive behavior has a shortfall to its presentation.

Reflexive behavior responds to the present while it is oblivious of the future. When the doctor hits my knee, my lower leg automatically reacts. You would think that, at my age, when I went to the doctor again, being fully aware of his former actions, the next time I saw him bring out that little instrument that I would press myself and tell my leg not to move when he taps because I know what he is getting ready to do. But no matter how many times I visit, when the doctor pulls out that instrument and hits me at that exact spot, my body automatically gives the same response.

It is the same if you start talking about Jesus. It doesn't matter how long it has been, you will get the same response out of me. When I start to think about the goodness of Jesus and all He has done for me, reflexively, something within me starts to leap for joy.

In dealing with desire, parents build in their children a discipline regimen of desire, which children ignorantly possess. For instance, a parent has to teach a young child to desire to brush his or her teeth. They will hold the toothbrush up to the child's mouth and make them brush. As the child gets older, the parents don't force the child any longer, but they give them an incentive by letting them know that they won't develop cavities or viruses if they brush their teeth. The child doesn't understand that when the parent was forcing them, they were helping them.

To force means to go against one's will, but in this case, it is to help them with something they didn't even understand. Probably God forced you to do some things that were uncomfortable for you, but you should understand that He took you through it because it helped you in the next season of your life. Maybe you had to bless those whom you knew were talking about you; maybe you had to smile at backstabbers; maybe you had to forgive those who tried to hurt you on purpose. God's response is that your response is going to reward you.

When children mature and develop, you can no longer force them to do what is required of them, but you will give them incentives instead. For example, you tell little Johnny, "If you do well in school, I will give you a Christmas present." The thing I love about God is that He is not above incentives. When God requires you to do something, expect a reward.

If you obey God, there are some things He will buy for you that you can't afford for yourself. You ought to have enough incentive to praise God, knowing that when the praises go up—the blessings come down. I don't know what is coming down, but it is better than what I have now, and that is enough incentive for me.

"There is a crown above your head that you have to grow tall enough to wear."
—Benjamin Elijah Mays

Benjamin Elijah Mays is attributed with saying that there is a crown above your head that you have to grow tall enough to wear.[3] I believe there is something you want from God that you know you can't afford, something you want God to do that seems virtually and naturally impossible. Maybe there is something you want God to provide that you don't have the education or the experience to supplement or support, but God wants you to desire Him first: *"Seek first the kingdom of God..."* (Matt. 6:33 NKJV).

In Matthew 22, we see an example of the pursuit of desire. We come across three wise men, also referred to as magi in the King James Version of the Bible. When Jesus was born, they saw a star in the East. They had to move from where they were to where Jesus was. However, there was a threat against their lives. Herod sought to kill them when all they were doing was trying to fulfill their desire. Prior to their search for God, no one was after them, but their decision to pursue and find the Savior ignited hatred in Herod.

You probably have never faced such attacks as you have lately, because you weren't seeking God as you are seeking Him now. Now that you are desperate to find God, opposition has appeared and everything has been trying to stop you. I don't know about you, but I have come from too far to let any devil or demonic pimps stop me from getting where I am trying to go—to find the face of God.

It can be argued that the wise men's desire was predicated on their environment. Notice that they were under a king, but it was not the earthly king they wanted. What happens when God gives you a desire to want something you already have? Some people are complacent with what they have, but there is a remnant who want the new anointing, a new blessing, and a new encounter with God.

The wise men were under attack because they were wise and gifted. You are already gifted, whether anyone ever gives you anything or not. There is something you are carrying that you didn't have to buy—because you were born with it. It doesn't matter what people try to do to you or say about you, they will never be able to be as gifted as you are. You *know* that you are gifted when you are on a fixed income, but your lights are still on. You are *really* gifted if you are raising your kids by yourself and they are still content and happy children.

> *My worship is not based on what I can get from God, but on what I can give God.*

The magi are believed to have worked for King Herod. They had a secure job until they started going after God. Then they faced attack from their supervisor because he had the position, but lacked the power. Herod recognized the gifting of the magi, but tried to block it. If your supervisor tries to do everything to step on your gift, understand that the job didn't make you, but you were gifted even before you went to the job. The magi's desire was to change their environment. They understood that if they could get to God through His earthly vessel, Jesus, everything around them would change. *If you can get to God, everything around you will change. Your desire ought to be to know God and not just to get something from Him. You are gifted with the ability to worship. The magi weren't concerned about what they could *get* from Jesus, but what they could bring *to* Him.

My worship is not based on what I can *get* from God, but on what I can *give* to God. The wise men used the express route to get to Jesus, and, when they arrived, they brought worship to Him, but they had to go home another way through detours. They went the long way, because if they had used the same route going back, what they'd escaped was still waiting to kill them.

God knows that it has taken you a long time to get what you desire, but the reason He couldn't let you get it quickly is because there are too many haters waiting to kill you and what He has for you. You take the long way to get what you desire so that when you finally get it, you remain safe. Maybe you went through imminent danger from your supervisor or people who want to see you dead, and it took you a long way and a long time just to get to where you are now. The Three Wise Men endured all the threats, the dangers, and the cold nights, because they had one desire—to worship God. They were wise men because they worshiped without a reward. It is your *job* to worship God because you were *created* to worship God; you were born to give *Him* glory.

God is looking for some wise people who know their gifting and who have a desire to worship in order to change their environments. If you are a wise person, I dare you to open your gifts and worship God. My one desire is not for God to make me debt free or famous, but for Him to allow me to see His face and to just worship Him. When you worship, God changes your environment.

ENDNOTES

1. A. A. Macdonell. *Hymns from the Rigveda* (Calcutta, London, 1922); *A Vedic Reader for Students* (Oxford, 1917).

2. Marvin Gaye, Nickolas Ashford & Valerie Simpson, 1966 for the Tamla Motown label

3. Benjamin Elijah Mays, http://www.morehouse .edu/admissions/home/pdf/2011-viewbook.pdf

Chapter 8

PAYMENT OF DESIRE

Your desire is going to cost you something. Desire can be dangerous when not ordained. Four of the most deadly sins, as recorded in Proverbs, are connected directly to desire: Envy, gluttony, lust, and greed. The remaining three; Sloth, wrath, and pride are indirectly connected to desire.

> There are six things the LORD hates, seven that are detestable to Him: haughty eyes, a lying tongue, hands that shed innocent blood, a heart that devises wicked schemes, feet that are quick to rush into evil, a false witness who pours out lies and a man who stirs up dissension among brothers (Proverbs 6:16-19).

Astute philosophers agree that the key to having a good life is to master desire. The question that looms then is: "How do I master desire?" Philosophers do not agree with Zen Buddhists, who suggest that to master a desire, all you have to do is meditate. They also don't agree with Christians, who pray when dealing with desire. Conversely, astute philosophers believe that to master desire people ought to pay close attention to what they desire and ask, "Why do I desire what I desire?"

There are probably some things in your life that you enjoyed and now regret because you didn't estimate the cost before undertaking them. Do you know how many people have made withdrawals out of your life without ever making a deposit? You are emptier because of your interaction with people to whom you gave so much of yourself to in order to make them happy, and they gave nothing back in return. As a result, you have ended up filing an emotional bankruptcy.

To move in a vicious cycle is a terrible thing—you spend all you have in a search for happiness and then still end up broke and unhappy. What then happens when you find yourself on a treadmill seeking happiness—always moving, but never making any progress? You become what Grace Jones calls "A slave to the rhythm,"[1] always trying to do something, but never really going anywhere.

In Mark 5, there was a man who was demon possessed. Jesus came over from the other side of the water and, after disembarking from the ship, met the demon-possessed man in the cemetery; the Latin word for cemetery or memorial is *memory*. In other words, the demon-possessed man was found in the place of memories. Most of the things that haunt you are not present-day incidents, but things from the past that you still remember. No wonder Paul the apostle said, *"Forgetting those things which are behind...I press toward the mark for the prize of the high calling"* (Phil. 3:13-14 KJV). You can recognize people who are still dealing with the past, because they are not in the posture to receive the present.

The demon-possessed man dealt with self-mutilation. People who are inflicting pain on themselves are injuring the outside because of an inward pain. When Jesus came to the man, the demons asked Christ why He had come to bother them ahead of schedule. There are some people who do not want God to disrupt their desire because they like it too much. But whenever God shows up, He comes to disrupt regularly-scheduled programs.

Anyone judging you based on your past is playing in your cemetery. God always shows up in the cemetery to let the devil know that the things he thought were dead are going to be resurrected. In the past, you probably have given up on a seemingly dead marriage, relationship, or financial situation. Don't ever stay in the cemetery—it is a place of hopelessness!

When you are confronted with physical circumstances beyond your control, the devil will mess you up with guilt and make you condemn yourself. Some of the stuff you are in is not even your doing, but rather what God is doing to you. Sometimes, God will put you in circumstances that are not comfortable or convenient, just to *test* your trust in Him. You don't have a desire until you have gone through a drought, and you don't know that you need something until you require it.

God wants you to have a need so that He can feel needed. If you have *everything*, then you don't *need* God. Just when it looks like life is coming together, God will take one piece of it away to see how long it will take you to call on Him or whether you will call on people, hoping that they will rescue you. An old songwriter said, "I need thee every hour, I need thee."[2] Some bills come just so that God can show off and prove to you that He is Jehovah Jireh—the Great Provider.

The Gospel of John tells a story of Mary and Martha, who had a brother called Lazarus. Lazarus was dying, and they sent for Jesus:

> *So the sisters sent word to Jesus, "LORD, the one You love is sick." When He heard this, Jesus said, "This sickness will not end in death. No, it is for God's glory so that God's Son may be glorified through it"* (John 11:3-4).

Jesus left Lazarus in his condition so that Mary and Martha would realize how much they needed God. There are people who don't understand why we spend most days in church when we *could* be shopping in the mall or out playing golf. The reason is simply because we have needs that other people can't meet.

A post-Hellenistic philosopher named Epictetus argued that we can't control everything because there are blows that come in life that we don't see coming. He advocates embracing the blows, suggesting that it will prevent them from hurting you.[3] Unfortunately, his philosophy is fatalistic in nature, because, according to him, whenever a trial or trauma comes, people don't have to act as if it fazes them, but act as if it was fate. I can't argue with that, because God and the enemy put me through circumstances.

There are some people who are satisfied with being broke, while, on the contrary, others refuse to settle for anything less and persistently ask God to change their lives. God can make you prosperous and happy like anyone else you admire.

Seneca argues that to overcome insatiability you have to know the difference between natural desire and unnatural desire.[4] When you are thirsty, you desire water, and that is a natural desire. Wealth, however, is not a natural desire, because although water can meet the

needs of thirst, acquiring wealth does not necessarily satisfy need, because you still need
more. If someone today gave you $100,000, you
would return after a month looking for another
$50,000, because there is no limit to wealth. God
enables people to know the difference between
natural and unnatural desires. Sin is a natural
desire in an unnatural context. Sex is not a bad
thing; it is a natural desire. But when a man
wants sex with another man, it is an unnatural
desire, and this makes it a sinful desire.

Sextus, an ancient Greek philosopher who
was born between 330 and 270 B.C., said that
much of our disappointment comes from
opinion.[5] You will never have your desires in
place until you get delivered from the opinions of other people. As long as you are living
to impress people, you will never be happy,
because what is in style today will be out of
style soon. Make up your mind to not *want*
based on the opinions of other people. You
were not born to impress people, but to give
God His glory.

Desire results from the seeking of a pleasure to escape pain. I hate needles, but if I
hypothetically catch the flu, I have to go to the

doctor and get a flu shot. Nobody makes me get the flu shot; rather, I willingly roll up my sleeve because I want to stay healthy. It hurts for a moment, but it will help me down the line. On the contrary, if I walked out of the hospital, and a mad, deranged assailant came from behind and stabbed me with a needle, the pain would be 100 times more exacerbated. It is the same physical pain, but the psychological pain would be much more severe, because the assailant was not trying to help me, but to hurt me.

When God brings pain into our lives, it is different from the pain of the enemy, because while it hurts for a season, God is trying to put something in us that will help us in the long run. Maybe some of the things that you went through this year hurt you; I am certain some could have even made you cry. It might have hurt, but you needed it in order to realize how powerful God is. It is after the pain that you are able to appreciate and thank God even more.

One of the lessons behind Lazarus' resurrection is that God will crush you to the place where you feel you are on the verge of death, just so He will get some glory. Some of the circumstances you are going through exist because God wants to see how long it is going to take you to give Him the praise in your pain. It is easy to praise Him when everything is good, but can you bless God when everything in your life is going wrong? Can praise really come out of you when every time you make progress, something pushes you three steps back?

> *Desire results from the seeking of a pleasure to escape pain.*

Do not fret because of evil men or be envious of those who do wrong; for like the grass they will soon wither, like green plants they will soon die away. Trust in the LORD and do good; dwell in the land and enjoy safe pasture. Delight yourself in the LORD and he will give you the desires of your heart (Psalm 37:1-4).

David the psalmist meant that before you are able to have your heart's desire, you need to first delight in the Lord. David starts by admonishing us to ignore our haters. Imagine if your haters don't like you even before you prosper; what will they do when God grants you all your desires? All your haters are going to be cut down.

In verse 3, David says that our desire should not be directed toward resources and all the stuff that is natural—rent, health insurance, transportation. God knows that we need them, and He promises to supply all our needs (see Phil. 4:19). When we remain faithful, God will not only give us what we need, but He will also meet all our wants.

How do you delight yourself in the Lord? You delight yourself in the Lord when it is the Lord who excites you, when nothing turns you on like being in the presence of God. It doesn't matter what car you drive; your ultimate excitement should arise because you know God and enjoy talking with Him. Sometimes, I find myself praying in the car without realizing it, simply because it is God who consumes me. You have to get to a place where you talk to God, not because you are in trouble or crisis, but just because you love His presence.

You delight yourself in the Lord when you enjoy giving to Him. People who don't love God enough get mad when asked to give, because they don't understand the Biblical principle that says, *"It is more blessed to give than to receive"* (Acts 20:35). I once went to a small church in North Carolina where the preacher called out 27 struggling single mothers to the altar for prayer. A man in the congregation who had never seen them before counted them and gave each a check for $1,000. The mothers started shouting because they had received the money, but Heaven was shouting because there was a man who had blessed them without demanding anything in exchange.

There is a blessing connected to anyone when they are able to be a blessing to someone else. I love giving to God, because God promises to match my giving with a 100-fold blessing. Luke 6:38 says:

> *Give, and it will be given to you. A good measure, pressed down, shaken together and running over, will be poured into your lap. For with the measure you use, it will be measured to you.*

Don't shout over what God gives to you, but celebrate whenever you have an opportunity to give something, because it's then that God opens the windows of Heaven. If you are a giver, then God qualifies and trusts you to become a getter. Anyone who is selfish is not a candidate for the overflow, but when you start giving, it is a sign of maturity. You are making room for new blessings.

I dream of the day when people will shout as fervently over giving as they do over receiving. If I backed off a truckload of new cars, people would rejoice, and I would make news, but what would it profit to have a new car without purpose? Don't look for what you can get from God, but what you can give to God, because every time you give to God, you get the unimaginable back. Sometimes the return is not tangible or material, but it could be perfect health in your body. Maybe you had a one-night stand unprotected, and you are HIV negative; you have favor on your life.

I love to sow because I know God gives back. Christmas today has somehow become demonized, because we look for what we can get instead of what we can give. It is unfortunate that we have bastardized the Lord's birth by looking for what we can get. At Christmas, God gave the ultimate, His Son, His very presence, and whoever has the Son in Him is blessed.

You delight yourself in the Lord when you praise God. I like praising, because I found out that the more I shout, the better I feel.

Whatever you desire will cost you something. In the natural, I define favor as "no money down," meaning, you achieve something without making a payment directly. It is time for God to give you the "big payback." God is preparing to bless you, not necessarily because you can't afford it on your own, but because God remembers how you prayed to Him, sowed, and tithed in your lack, and how you praised Him when you were tired. Now God is going to meet your needs as a reminder that you are not forgotten.

> *However, as it is written: "No eye has seen, no ear has heard, no mind has conceived what God has prepared for those who love Him"* (1 Corinthians 2:9).

God wants us to get excited about Him, as Solomon puts it in Song of Songs 7:10: *"I belong to my lover, and his desire is for me."* It is God's desire for you to have what you want, and those who do not rejoice in your success do not please God.

ENDNOTES

1. Grace Jones, *Slave to the Rhythm*. Trevor Horn. 1985.

2. Hawks, Annie S., *I Need Thee Every Hour* hymn (1872)

3. Epictetus, *The Enchiridion*, Translated by Elizabeth Carter. The Internet Classics Archive by Daniel C. Stevenson, Web Atomics.© 1994-2000, Daniel

4. L. Annaeus Seneca, *On Benefits*, Book 7

5. Sextus Empiricus, *Outlines of Pyrrhonism*, Book One, Cambridge, Massachusstes, 1933, translated by R.G. Bury

Chapter 9

PATTERN OF DESIRE

One thing I have desired of the Lord, that will I seek: that I may dwell in the house of the LORD all the days of my life, to behold the beauty of the LORD, and to inquire in His temple (Psalm 27:4 NKJV).

Our desires can be categorized according to reason or importance. Sometimes we want something, not for itself, but to get us closer to another desire. If you drive to a restaurant to get something to eat, you do not necessarily desire to drive or to visit the restaurant, but you probably just desire something to eat. Therefore, the driving and the restaurant are just the means to the end. If someone were to ask or interview you on why you drove to the restaurant, your response would probably be because you needed something to eat to relieve your hunger. In asking those questions, you examine, calculate, interpret, and dissect why you do what you do.

In life, there are things we want just because they connect us to what we really desire. For example, in some relationships, it might not be true that we want the person we are with, but really what that person represents. Maybe we do not really want our job, but rather the paycheck that is connected to the job.

> *The enemy traps many of us to confuse our desires with our destination.*

A German philosopher once said that we categorize wealth by deeming we are wealthy as long as we make a $100 more than our neighbor. The enemy traps many of us to confuse our desires with our destination. Once we have attained one goal, we think that it is the end of what God has in store for us. As a result, we keep looking in vain for the next level of excitement, acceptance, and approval.

Most drug addicts did not start on heroin, but on alcohol. When the drink was not enough to get them high, they had to find something stronger, and if that failed, too, they sought something more intense. Even in dealing with sexual addicts, addiction did not start with intercourse, but possibly with a sexually-rated show on television that their parents warned them against. They gave into watching out of curiosity, and thus, desire was accelerated.

TYPES OF DESIRE

There are two different types of desire:

- Instrumental desire

- Terminal desire (hedonistic or non-hedonistic)

Instrumental desire is when we desire something for the sake of something else, while terminal desire is when we desire something for its own sake. Some people use worship as an instrumental desire by worshipping God just to receive blessings. Our worship ought to be terminal, in that we worship God not because we want something from Him, but just because we enjoy giving Him the glory. Other people give compliments as an instrument to get to something terminal. God is looking for a generation of believers who are not worshipping Him because they want to get something from Him, but because they realize who He is.

Under terminal desire, there is the hedonistic desire and non-hedonistic desire. In hedonistic desire, people like something because it makes them feel good and satisfied. Non-hedonistic desire is when people don't benefit from a desire, but just enjoy doing it. For example, I eat because I desire to satisfy my hunger. However, when I am full, my hedonistic desire, which the Lord called gluttony, steps in. I will continue to eat—not because I need to—but because I like doing it. Some of the sins we commit are a result of routine and not enjoyment.

God shifts our desires by getting us to a place where the things that used to excite us now turn us off. In relation to desire, our activities in worship determine our response to what we encounter in the world. For example, desire is an emotion that has an expression. Sometimes we praise God even when we don't feel like it, because we understand that God will change our circumstances in the midst of praise. At times, I wake up a little bit depressed, stressed, and burnt out, but the more I praise God, the better I feel.

---

*The motivation of desire
speaks to the level of desire.*

Sometimes, desire goes against your will and submits to one that is beyond your control. Sometimes desire will have you start doing things that you had not preprogrammed yourself to do. When you are crazy in love, you are "forced" to spend money on someone who, if you were in your right mind, you wouldn't have gone broke over. If something happened to the person whom you are madly in love with, you would go to their house at 3:00 A.M. just to help or do anything you could, but as time passed and your feelings changed, in similar circumstances, you might choose not to respond in the same way. It is because God changed your desire.

Probably there is something you've always desired to have, but now that you have had some setbacks and disappointments, you've made up your mind to live without it. If you have God on your side, you can make it through the rough times.

The motivation of desire speaks to the level of desire. You have to ask yourself critically and analytically, *Why do I want what I want?* Do you want because you really need it or because everybody else has it? When you ask God for what you desire, don't base your request on what others have, but, instead, demand what is uniquely designed to suit your needs. Just as people would search for lost car keys, not because they want the keys, but because they desire to drive the car, likewise, when we seek God, we seek to find protection and direction in Him.

People without desire are those whom psychologists deem as depressed. People without desire are incapable of expressing feelings. They lack hedonistic or non-hedonistic terminal desires, but have non-hedonistic impulses—always unmotivated. Probably people you know are going through a season where the enemy has them in a chokehold—not desiring anything. Maybe they have become apathetic and complacent with life without any hope of ever getting better.

You will know that you are surrounded by non-hedonistic people if, whenever you try to improve yourself, they become threatened. Some people will get mad when they see you blessed, because they enjoy seeing you stagnant. Unfortunately, they don't understand that even if you don't have the promise, you are walking in the manifestation of what God has in store for you.

People who are not motivated slip into depression, because they don't have the desire, the will, or the drive to expect more for their lives. King David was about to be swept away by depression and overrun by anxiety when Saul wanted to kill him. David encouraged himself and knew that he would not die, but would live to fulfill his purpose on earth (see 1 Sam. 30:6). You do not decide, but discover your desire through experience and exposure. You never know what you want until you've seen it.

The problem with the devil is that he lets us see and covet the wealth of the wicked. God wants us to look at their wealth, not as an incentive to anger, but rather as a possibility. We have to learn how to decipher and discipline our desires. We also have to know where we have to go to have our desires met.

> *One thing I have desired of the LORD, that will I seek: that I may dwell in the house of the LORD all the days of my life, to behold the beauty of the LORD and to inquire in His temple* (Psalm 27:4 NKJV).

"One thing have I desired," is a decision. It is something David wanted for himself, not because someone had placed it upon his life. *"Of the Lord…"* is a discovery. David didn't want his need from other people, because he understood that people would let him down.

"I may dwell in the house of the Lord," is instrumental desire. David didn't just want to *visit* the presence of God, but to *dwell* in His

presence, praising and worshipping always. *"To behold the beauty of the Lord,"* is terminal desire. In other words, David meant that his desires were so intact that he knew what he wanted, whom he needed, and where to find his desires.

My mother is from Yankees, New York, 245 North Broadway, straight out of the "hood." She was raised along with nine others by my grandmother in a two-bedroom apartment. None of them were on drugs, none ever spent a night in jail, and none ever broke the law. While growing up, my mother never experienced the ordeal of a commercial Christmas, and as a consequence, when I was growing up, every Christmas we would get into the car, and I would think we were going Christmas shopping.

Instead, my mother would have my father drive us through Green Spring Station just to see houses that had lights. We didn't know anyone who lived in the houses, but my mother just wanted to see the lights—even if she couldn't go in. She didn't know the owners of the houses, but she liked what was on the outside of the houses. She said, "I don't have to own the house; I just want to see its beauty." When I visit church, I just want to see the glory of God and the effulgence of His power, not the people or the clothes they wear.

The pivotal and probing question is: What is your desire? If nothing ever happens, your desire ought to be to see the face of God in worship. God's glory will change your desire for people, acceptance, and approval.

———————————

As I conclude this chapter, not long ago, all of America found itself at a startling standstill with the capture and then the killing of Osama bin Laden. What many people do not know is that in the inception of this embryonic terrorist mind, his focus was not the United States; it was the Soviet Union. It was his desire to rid the world of communism. However, after America went into the Persian Gulf for war in 1992, his desire changed to no longer deal with communism, but to deal with democracy. Osama Bin Laden was right in one thing; he changed desires, but his desire still was under a violent undercurrent.

In this last chapter, I hope you will change desires. But if you are going to change desires, you also need to change methodology, because if your methodology doesn't change, then your desire is still the same.

ABOUT DR. JAMAL HARRISON BRYANT

In every generation, God selects a leader with a voice to empower his people; Jamal Harrison Bryant is that voice for this generation that speaks a language that can be understood in the streets and the sanctuary. He believes that his voice is to empower people socially, spiritually, economically, and educationally and to enrich them culturally.

Dr. Jamal Harrison Bryant must be one of the lead voices for this generation, attracting up to 12,000 of the most difficult generation to reach (which is 18-43 years of age) in under 10 years. He started in his living room with a Bible study, moved to a college auditorium, and then to a high school. Now he pastors one church in two locations.

A voice that is recognized on TBN, BET, and TV One, he is also the first pastor serving as a spiritual voice on reality television, having been featured on "K-Ci and Jo-Jo Come Clean" and "Omarosa's Ultimate Merger."

What an incredible voice that can testify about failing the 11th grade, getting a GED, and then moving on to graduate from More-house College with a bachelor's degree in Political Science and International Studies. He also received a master's degree in divinity from Duke University, and achieved a doctor-ate degree in theology from Oxford University in England.

He has a clear voice that speaks globally, having established a church in West Africa, two charter Schools (one in Baltimore and another in Liberia), a family life center, and a Youth Development Center; he also gives over $100,000 annually in scholarships for education.

He is also a compassionate voice that sent 17,000 pair of shoes to Haiti after the earthquake, gave $100,000 to Hurricane Katrina victims, has preached across the United States, Europe, Africa, the Caribbean, India, and Australia. Christian Book Retailers recognize him as a 2010 bestseller and African American Publishers recognizes him as the author of the year with the 2010 African American Nonfiction Literacy Award, for his book World War Me—a testimony of his failures and his favor.

His is an empowering voice that uses the Word to change the world. No matter whether you are 7 or 70, once you've heard it, you will never forget the voice of Jamal Harrison Bryant.

Other Exciting Books by
Dr. Jamal Harrison Bryant

Foreplay

Finding Yourself In Scripture

Everything You Need From A–Z

World War Me

IN THE RIGHT HANDS, THIS BOOK WILL CHANGE LIVES!

Most of the people who need this message will not be looking for this book. To change their lives, you need to put a copy of this book in their hands.

> *But others (seeds) fell into good ground, and brought forth fruit, some a hundred-fold, some sixty-fold, some thirty-fold* (Matthew 13:8).

Our ministry is constantly seeking methods to find the good ground, the people who need this anointed message to change their lives. Will you help us reach these people?

> *Remember this—a farmer who plants only a few seeds will get a small crop. But the one who plants generously will get a generous crop* (2 Corinthians 9:6).

EXTEND THIS MINISTRY BY SOWING
3 BOOKS, 5 BOOKS, 10 BOOKS, OR MORE TODAY,
AND BECOME A LIFE CHANGER!

Thank you,

Don Nori Sr., Founder
Destiny Image
Since 1982